LOST INTIMACIES

gender & culture
sexuality

William J. Spurlin
General Editor

Vol. 4

PETER LANG
New York • Washington, D.C./Baltimore • Bern
Frankfurt am Main • Berlin • Brussels • Vienna • Oxford

William J. Spurlin

LOST INTIMACIES

Rethinking Homosexuality
under National Socialism

PETER LANG
New York • Washington, D.C./Baltimore • Bern
Frankfurt am Main • Berlin • Brussels • Vienna • Oxford

Library of Congress Cataloging-in-Publication Data
Spurlin, William J.
Lost intimacies: rethinking homosexuality under national socialism /
William J. Spurlin.
p. cm. — (Gender, sexuality, and culture; v. 4)
Includes bibliographical references and index.
1. Gays—Nazi persecution. 2. National socialism and homosexuality.
3. Gays—Germany—Identity. I. Title.
D804.5.G38S68   306.76'6094309043—dc22   2008019403
ISBN 978-0-8204-7892-0
ISSN 1528-6525

Bibliographic information published by **Die Deutsche Bibliothek**.
Die Deutsche Bibliothek lists this publication in the "Deutsche
Nationalbibliografie"; detailed bibliographic data is available
on the Internet at http://dnb.ddb.de/.

Cover design by Joni Holst
Cover images: The pink marble inverted triangle commemorating homosexual victims
of National Socialism, located at Nollendorfplatz, Berlin (the translation of the inscription reads:
"Struck dead and silenced: The homosexual victims of National Socialism").
This image is superimposed on "Shalechet—Gefallenes Laub" ("Fallen Leaves")
by Menashe Kadishman located in one of the five voids of the Jüdisches Museum, Berlin.
Photographs taken by the author.

© 2009 Peter Lang Publishing, Inc., New York
29 Broadway, 18th floor, New York, NY 10006
www.peterlang.com

All rights reserved.
Reprint or reproduction, even partially, in all forms such as microfilm,
xerography, microfiche, microcard, and offset strictly prohibited.

pour Madame Ana Markey

and for David,
again, again, and again...

Acknowledgments

I would like to express my deepest thanks and gratitude to those whose generous assistance enabled me to complete this book. I am very grateful to colleagues who read the entire manuscript, in whole or in parts, or read various papers from the larger work. Their considered suggestions and responses were invaluable; especially Phyllis Lassner at Northwestern University, Chris Weedon at Cardiff University, Pierre Zoberman at Paris XIII, Debbie Epstein at University College, London, and Cardiff University, Alan Sinfield at the University of Sussex, and Marcia Blumberg at York University in Toronto.

I am especially grateful to the British Arts and Humanities Research Council (AHRC) for partially funding this project through a Research Leave Grant in 2004. Along with a sabbatical given at Cardiff University, this grant enabled me to extend my sabbatical to a full year and complete most of the major research for this project. I also wish to thank the various professional organizations that provided me with forums in which to discuss my work in progress for this book and receive feedback; these include the Twentieth-Century Comparative Literature Division of the Modern Language Association through the session organized by Margaret Higonnet "Wars Others"; the American Comparative Literature Association, where I was able to organize a one-day seminar "Dissidence/Decadence: Comparative Sexualities at the *Fin de Siècle*," along with Gail Finney, Jennifer Burns Levin, Roxana M. Verona, Elizabeth Richmond-Garza, and Noriko Hiraishi; and the International Society for the History of Rhetoric. I also give heartfelt thanks to Pierre Zoberman for the opportunity to give a plenary paper on the topic of this book at the conference he organized at Paris XIII in 2005 to initiate the new Centre pour les études des nouveaux espaces littéraires. A revised and extended version of that paper will soon be published as an essay entitled "'*Rein bleiben und reif warden!*': Nazisme et racialisation du désir homoérotique," in *Queer: Écritures de la différence? Autres temps, autres lieux* (ed. Pierre Zoberman; Paris: L'Harmattan, 2008). I am grateful for permission granted to recontextualize that material here and use it in English. Both delivering the paper and writing the longer essay in French not only situated further this project in comparative studies, but enabled me to work in the often contested spaces between languages and thereby think through many of my theoretical and critical assumptions, which then became an important impetus for revision.

I would like to thank the librarians at the various libraries and archives at which I worked for their endless patience in helping me to find often difficult to locate sources. In particular, I would like to thank the staff at the library and archive at the United States Holocaust Memorial Museum (USHMM) in Washington, DC, and I appreciate those who showed interest in my work at the Centre for Advanced Holocaust Studies at the USHMM. I also appreciated the kind assistance of the librarians and staff at the Bibliothèque Nationale de France (BNF) in Paris, especially those who allowed me to photocopy materials slightly beyond the allotted limits! The librarians at the Humboldt University libraries in Berlin were extremely helpful, especially in the history and philosophy collections. And closer to home, the librarian staff at the British Library in London, as always, were extremely helpful, as they were in the libraries at Cardiff and Sussex Universities. I am also grateful to colleagues and graduate students from the English Graduate Colloquium Series at the University of Sussex for their feedback and support when I gave a colloquium paper in that forum based on chapter 3 of this book. My colleagues and graduate students in the Centre for the Study of Sexual Dissidence & Cultural Change at Sussex are highly valued for their patience and understanding when sometimes the completion of this book momentarily had to overtake other priorities.

I would like also to thank Phyllis Korper, my editor at Peter Lang in New York, who was also editor for my very first book in 1995 *The New Criticism and Contemporary Literary Theory: Connections and Continuities* (co-edited with Michael Fischer) when she worked for Taylor and Francis. While she retired just before the completion of this book, her support for it and for the Series on Gender, Sexuality, and Culture was unwavering throughout her tenure, and it was a joy to work with her. And I thank Bernie Shade and her staff at Peter Lang for all of their hard work in the time-consuming production process.

Last, but never least, I thank my partner, David A. Smith, for his continuing love and support, despite what must have seemed my perpetual state of pre-occupation with this project. In 2005, in the midst of writing this book, we registered for our civil partnership in London. This gave me pause at the time to consider deeply another kind of public registration on the social ledger for homosexuals in nazi Germany and so many same-sex intimacies and lives lost under the Third Reich…and often forgotten. It is hoped that this book will help to incite further discussion and debate about this particular history in their memory.

London
W.J.S.

Table of Contents

Acknowledgments   vii
General Editor's Foreword   xi

Introduction   1

CHAPTER 1   Holocaust Studies Meets Queer Studies: A Contested Alliance?   15

CHAPTER 2   The Racialization of Sexuality: Rethinking Same-Sex Desire within Nazi Juridical Discourse   29

CHAPTER 3   The Politics of Gender Difference: Lesbian Existence under the Third Reich   45

CHAPTER 4   Homosexuality and Fascism: A (Re)Analysis   65

CHAPTER 5   Discursive Traces of Nazi Homophobia in Contemporary Culture   85

CHAPTER 6   Queer Sexuality, Holocaust Studies, and the Challenge of Democratic Futurity   109

Notes   121
References   139
Index   147

General Editor's Foreword

In the contemporary world, we have come to understand gender and sexuality as shifting sites of signification. Unlike their traditional constructions tied to the expression of an inner self or essence under a humanist paradigm, postmodern theory, feminism, and academic queer theory have enabled radical rethinking of gender and sexuality as multiple, fluid, variable, contingent, and contextual as they operate under a variety of cultural, historical, rhetorical, and ideological conditions. These fields of inquiry have also helped to denaturalize any causal, normative relation proffered *between* gender and sexuality, exposing these relations as political and deeply imbricated within a heteronormative social order. In particular, academic queer theory, as a mode of analysis and critique, and with its emphasis on the proliferation of social differences, has helped to challenge identic fixity and has enabled more complex theorizations of gender and sexual identity in relation to other sites of subjective identification, including—but not limited to—race, class, geopolitical spatialization, and national affiliation.

This series is a forum for the critical investigation and analysis of the contested terrain between culture, gender, and sexuality. The books collected in the series are productive of new directions in queer studies and gender studies as they critically examine the relation(s) between culture and gender and/or sexuality in a range of historical periods. Some projects retheorize gender in relation to, or its constitution through, sexuality, race, class, or culture. Other books are studies of sexuality and sexual identity that produce new understandings of gender or are broad inquiries into culture that raise compelling implications for the ways in which we think about gender and sexuality as we begin a new century.

While the series has been influenced by a previous decade productive of queer theorizing, the lines of inquiry undertaken in its aftermath by the authors collected here are both numerous and exciting. For instance, more comparative work and further analyses of gender and sexuality in postcolonial contexts will enable critique of the Euroamerican biases of gender and queer inquiry, while calling attention to their undertheorization in postcolonial studies to the extent that gender and sexuality often remain contained within heteronormative frames of reference. The breaking down of national borders, made possible by heightened diasporic migration, the impact of economic globalization, the rapid dissemination of texts and culture worldwide, and the explosion of information technology further impinge on our traditional understandings of gender and sexuality while continuing to radically transform them. The books in this series represent highly theoretical engagements with gender and sexuality through a broad range of interdisciplinary inquiry, including anthropology, literary studies, history, psychology, and other areas of the humanities and social sciences. Each volume, as well as the series as a whole, will make a unique contribution to furthering our understanding of gender and sexuality as categories of analysis and their complex and multiple configurations in the vast, historically specific network(s) of codes, symbols, and signifying practices we have come to understand as culture.

William J. Spurlin
University of Sussex

Introduction

As high school students in fourth-year French in Turnersville, New Jersey, during the 1970s, we had an amazing European teacher who taught us the plays of Molière, the *Confessions* of Rousseau and *Émile ou de l'Education*, the poetry of Rimbaud and Baudelaire…all in French, of course. She often took us to New York to museums, theaters, and French restaurants to make French literature and culture come alive for us. Being a very small, but very special, class of final-year French students, "Madame" made us feel very continental and so sophisticated. We couldn't quite name it then, but other students, and even her own colleagues, regarded her as a bit odd, as someone who didn't quite fit. But it was precisely her eccentricity that attracted those of us in her class to her; in fact, when I later taught in Singapore between finishing my undergraduate work and starting graduate school, I often hoped that my students there would see me as "foreign" and "interesting" in the same way that we had seen Madame. But we never knew until the end of our final year of high school French that Madame had actually witnessed the brutalities of nazism while starting to study for her law examinations as a young graduate student in Paris. Her husband at the time was in the Resistance, and while she was away at a library studying in the very early days of the German occupation, she returned to find that her husband had been taken away by nazi officials without a trace, and she never saw him again. A few days later, she and her mother were fortunate enough to secure air tickets and board an Air France flight to the United States. Madame recounted how people on the plane actually wept when the pilot announced that the plane had left French air space, because it meant, she told us, "*de ce temps ils étaient libre.*"

This was, for many of my small group of fellow French students, our first encounter with the Holocaust. Madame was odd, somewhat exotic, and perhaps a little "queer" in the sense that no other teacher we had was anything like her. A bit later in the 1970s, the series *Holocaust* was televised, and films such as *QB VII* chronicled the persecution of nazi criminals after the war. European history courses at university seemed to gloss over this crucial part of history by mentioning the deportations and the internments at camps rather matter-of-factly. It wasn't until the early 1980s and my own coming out—first to myself, then socially, and later academically—that I began to read the accounts of gay men who were victims of the Third Reich. But I could never forget that someone whom I had admired and identified with, and who had had such dedication and pride in her work, could have been a victim of nazi power as a Jewish woman some thirty plus years before teaching us high school honors French, and could possibly have been taken away herself had she been at home when the nazis came for her young husband. And as I began to take up gay studies following my graduate work in the early 1990s, the question of outsiderness, disbelonging, queerness stayed with me in relation to Madame's story and in relation to such little documentation on the positions of gay men and lesbians under nazism and in the Holocaust in general. Yet when I started researching this in Holocaust studies, initially dabbling here and there (I wasn't a historian, after all), I soon learned that a focus on queer sexuality was regarded as...well...rather taboo.

Fast-forward to 2004. While researching this book on a year-long sabbatical, part of which was spent at the library of the United States Holocaust Memorial Museum (USHMM) in Washington, D.C., I quickly learned after my arrival that the Center for Advanced Holocaust Studies at the museum had organized a one-day academic public symposium on gender and the Holocaust. I was thrilled at the fortunate coincidence in timing. Such a symposium could bring new and exciting perspectives to bear on Holocaust research and also perhaps inform my own thinking, since I was myself researching a very similar, highly politicized topic. Moreover, since I was still rather new to the area of Holocaust studies—as one trained in comparative literature and critical theory and working in queer studies—the symposium would be a rare treat. It would allow me the privilege of simply sitting in the audience and taking it all in without the usual pressures that typically surround academic conferences in terms of preparing and delivering a paper, organizing and chairing panels, committee work, and so on. (I was on sabbatical, after all!) I immediately signed myself up and arrived early on the afternoon of the symposium so as to get a good seat in the auditorium.

There were about 8–10 panelists in all from all parts of the United States and one or two from Europe—papers ranging from such topics as abortion and sterilization, pregnancy in non-Aryan women, the testimonies of female survivors in camps, the ways in which Jewish women in the ghettos created new bonds and strategies for survival, reproductive capability in Jewish women as a site of endangerment as compared to Jewish men, and the effects of the lived experiences of displacement and separation from children and spouses on women's lives. It was fascinating. My mind raced with implications the papers raised for an analysis of sexuality and sexual difference, as my research to date had already taught me that sexuality, within the context of National Socialism, could not be regarded as a separate axis of analysis apart from race and anti-Semitism.

Eager to participate, my hand shot up during the question-and-answer period; I felt almost like one of my own over-eager students. But the moderator called upon two elderly gentlemen, one right after the other, by name, both of whom were rather eminent scholars in the field and obviously well known by the museum's Center for Advanced Holocaust Studies. The first respondent complimented the panelists on their "interesting" papers but wondered aloud what possible relevance such a political focus on a topic like gender had remotely to do with the Holocaust. He then waited for a response. A stinging silence followed; a few audible gasps could be heard in the audience…then silence again. The panelists, rather exasperated from just having given their papers and then having this as their first question, huddled among themselves to formulate a response to this rather hostile question posed under the guise of academic politeness. Panelists who had spoken most directly on the extermination of Jewish women, and the ways in which non-Aryan women were subject to the control of nazi reproduction politics, pointed to the implications of their research for understanding the Holocaust as a distinct event in history, and they backed up their statements impeccably with historical sources. Audience members defended the panelists in arguing that the discipline had for too long been dominated by men and already had a masculinist slant to it, proven by virtue of the question that had just been asked. Others noted that the panelists opened up new questions and refreshing perspectives for Holocaust studies. One brave panelist asked the audience to take note of the politics of gender operating within the very forum itself, as all but one of the panelists were female. Such a question, she continued, would never have come up had the panel been comprised entirely, or predominately, of men, and if the topic had not been about gender.

What does the politics of gender have to do with the Holocaust indeed?! The question both puzzled and concerned me. On the one hand, it seemed very much like the questions asked about literature, history, and the arts and humanities in general more than a decade ago, at which time questions of race, gender, sexuality, class, and imperialism enabled new ways of looking at texts and at culture beyond aesthetic, positivistic, or formalistic approaches, but had created controversy among more traditional humanists who preferred that such political issues be kept safely at bay. Yet this, too, was a form of silencing, not indistinct from the question asked at the Holocaust symposium on gender, because such critiques lack an interrogation of their own politics to the extent that they try to keep politicized questions outside the boundaries of disciplinary inquiry. More concerning, however, is that the gentleman's question regarding the relevance of gender could be quite easily applied to sexuality; that is, taking the implications of his position further, a focus on sexuality could not provide any viable narratives on the historical period of the Third Reich or on the study of the Holocaust.

Narratives of sexuality began to appear in the early 1980s as testimony written by gay men who had survived the nazi period and wrote about their own persecution and that of other homosexuals. These narratives fostered a general concern in Holocaust studies that a focus on homosexuality might occlude the Jewish significance of the Holocaust insofar as other victims of nazi persecution were not necessarily doomed for annihilation by virtue of "who they were" as were Jewish victims. Prior to the establishment of gender and queer studies in the academy, scholarship on gender or sexuality may have been deemed risky and not very rigorous, which is obviously still a prejudice in the field of Holocaust studies, given the comment made at the symposium as late as 2004 and at the U.S. Holocaust Memorial Museum. Another concern has been that a focus on sexuality may be so titillating for audiences, readers of scholarship, and students who study the Holocaust that the intensity and depth of human suffering could be trivialized. For example, as Elizabeth Heineman notes, might an exploration of sexuality help us better understand genocide or possibly serve a pornographic function and titillate the reader, thereby making the study of genocide appealing? Citing Omer Bartov, she notes that Israeli youth, "the literal and figurative children of the survivors," were titillated and not merely sobered by the images of sexual sadism and nudity in the camps (54–55).[1] These concerns indicate that an entrenched conservatism regarding the representation of sexuality in Holocaust literature and scholarship is by no means to be relegated to the past as a form of old-fashioned thinking. Yet, as Heineman qualifies, problematic modes of representation and reception cannot be confused with serious attempts to understand the ways in which genocide and sexuality may intersect. It would simply be bad scholarship to ignore evidence that appears consistently in the historical record (55) and that may be subject to new interpretation when addressed by a range of social, historical, and theoretical questions that continue to shape the cultural and historical significance of the Holocaust.

Other work on sexuality has sought to explain fascism by conflating it with homosexual desire insofar as the hypermasculinity projected by nazi power appealed to a submissive and/or masochistic personality type in some nazi men who were supposedly seduced by fascism's homoerotic appeal. Such men were not necessarily homosexual, given the intensity of the homosocial bonds required and the simultaneous disavowal of their homoerotic potential, especially with Hitler's 1941 decision to prescribe the death penalty for homosexuality within the ranks of the SS and Secret Police, which I shall discuss in chapter 4. Nonetheless, for now I would like to note that any conflation of homosexuality with fascism once again reduces homosexuality to a symptom and to the source of fascism. Such an approach also recenters heteronormative relations and reproduces the dominant psychoanalytic grid of gender whereby hegemonic masculinity is based on the repudiation of femininity unconsciously associated with castration. Moreover, since gay and lesbian victims of the Holocaust have struggled to be recognized as such, these studies potentially convert homosexuals from the status of victims to the more or less equivalent status as the fascist perpetrators themselves.

Yet despite the appearance of testimonies from gay men, and later from lesbian victims, research using same-sex desire as a lens of inquiry into the Holocaust has remained marginal. As Günter Grau writes:

> A conscious attempt to link the sociohistorical environment for homosexuality and homosexual men and women in the Third Reich to what Dirk Blasius calls the "broader context of historical process" has not been identified. For the most part, relevant research projects have been treated separately from one another. In reappraising this special part of German history, there has been a general lack of conceptualization of the matter as a distinct and important issue. (338)[2]

While this was the case up until a few years ago, recent work has begun to address sexuality seriously as imbricated in nazi power, focusing both on heterosexuality and homosexuality and providing new insights into cultural and social organization under the Third Reich. For example, challenging stereotypes of the nazis as prudish and as guardians of good taste and pristine morals, Dagmar Herzog, in her article in a special issue of the *Journal of the History of Sexuality* in 2002, and in her recent book *Sex after Fascism*, points out that only in one sense was nazism a backlash against the more progressive sexual mores and proclivities of the Weimar that preceded it (that is, in terms of homosexuality and the growing preoccupation with sex). However, as Herzog continues, the nazis also redefined, expanded, and intensified—rather than fully suppressed—the inheritance of sexually liberalizing tendencies from the early part of the twentieth century as the privilege of non-disabled, heterosexual Aryans (*Sex after Fascism* 5). Herzog also reads the social and sexual conservatism of German postwar culture not as a continuation of nazi prudery but as a partial reaction against the liberal sexual morality of nazism (*Sex after Fascism* 3). *Sex after Fascism* is a study of twentieth-century German cultural history through the various shifts and conflicts over sexual morality. Herzog goes on to question dominant readings of New Left politics in 1960s West Germany that interpreted the sexual politics of the Third Reich as profoundly repressive. She sees the New Left's attempt to liberate sexuality as a way of cleansing Germany of the after-effects of nazism as misdirected, because the New Left was really responding to the postwar culture of sexual conservatism that *followed* nazism (*Sex after Fascism* 2).

Other work, as Gregor, Roemer, and Roseman point out in the introduction to their 2006 *German History from the Margins*, sees debates about sex, within the framework of nationalism or nation building, as an important axis of investigation to the extent that it resonates deeply with anxieties about the nation and its purity and violability (15). Certainly this was true under nazism with regard to its obsessions with racial purity and the elimination of social degeneracy, with the threats posed to these nationalist goals impugned to Jews and homosexuals through the racialization of homosexuality and the (homo)sexualization of Jews, a point I shall discuss further in chapter 2. Yet Gregor, Roemer, and Roseman also argue that it is important not to read those marked by the nation with the sign of otherness as mere social outsiders, because those relegated to the margins also engaged the center and altered its contours and character. This means that the center cannot necessarily remain homogeneous, unaffected by the margins, as is often assumed by theories of nationalism, but is more fluid and tenuous (2). These points are precisely those that informed my own recent book *Imperialism within the Margins: Queer Representation and the Politics of Culture in Southern Africa*, also published in 2006. One particular impetus for writing the current book was to revise the interrogatory optic somewhat and ask how African cultural nationalism in both settler (Afrikaner) and indigenous cultures in South Africa, and attempts at the erasures of (sexual) difference as part of a project to form a harmonious national culture and identity that is distinct from the last vestiges of colonial influence (such as homosexuality, often regarded as alien to indigenous culture), may shed further light on German nationalism under the Third Reich, while acknowledging, of course, that one context is not reducible to the other.

Interestingly, there is a link with South Africa that is more direct. In researching my previous book, I found that the Afrikaner framers of apartheid in South Africa were very well versed in theories of scientific racism coming out of Europe and in the racial theories of nazism in the 1930s. In fact, as Barbara Bush notes in *Imperialism, Race and Resistance*, the developing trend toward German fascism was imbricated with the spectacle of the 1938 centenary celebration of the Great Trek, which glorified not only the Afrikaners' pioneering heritage in images of covered ox-wagons moving across South Africa, but their creed of racial purity and white destiny (140). Moreover, as Anne McClintock argues, the images of the Great Trek, which asserted Afrikaner independence from British laws under colonialism (including the whip-wielding patriarch on horseback, black servants toiling alongside, and the women inside the covered ox-wagons in their starched white bonnets signifying the purity of the race), were powerful constructions of racial and gender differences, with women representing the moral and spiritual mission of the *Volk*, and men its political and economic agency (*Imperial Leather* 371). Yet at the same time, these powerful representations of Afrikaner nationalism, through the idealization of male/female bonds and the centering of the nuclear heterosexual family, also served to reinforce heteronormative social relations defensively, so much so that race, gender, and sexuality were inextricably linked.

To what extent, then, might nationalist discourses in South Africa, given its apartheid past, and the marking of same-sex desire as alien to both indigenous and settler cultures and histories, shed light on nazi power and its attempt to construct a new nation and empire?[3] *Moreover, what assumptions of sexuality are built into both regimes that tried to maintain racial purity and national integrity?* This is not to reduce postcolonial nationalism to nazi fascism, but is to engage the ways in which certain tropes and practices of social and cultural organization attempt to redefine the nation and a new sense of national belonging, using (homo)sexuality as an organizing principle despite concurrent claims as to its aberrant status within the nationalist frame. In this regard, postcolonial studies has sent me back to Europe to question further the relationship between race and sexuality in the context of formative discourses of nationhood during the Third Reich. This project is more specifically focused on asking how anti-homophobic inquiry, as a mode of analysis and critique, can be used to more systematically and more explicitly theorize the politics of sexuality, specifically same-sex desire and state-sanctioned homophobia under nazism. This question is approached with the clear recognition that homophobia seldom operated alone, but operated in conjunction with other axes of power (as it did under colonialism and continues in postcolonial nationalist imaginaries), including race, gender, and particular national policies, which under the Third Reich included eugenics and population politics.

With these thoughts in mind, then, this book critically analyzes the social and cultural construction of gay and lesbian identity and homophobia under nazism. Care is taken not to examine queer desire and nazi homophobia as separate categories distinct from the insistent pressures of other axes of subjectification and power, and to ensure that an analysis of sexual difference does not occur apart from the wider historical context of nazi social policies pertaining to race and reproductive and population politics. The book also regards gender and sexuality as entangled axes of analysis as a way of allowing the specificity of lesbian difference to emerge, a topic that has not been examined widely in historical research on the period or in Holocaust studies. The book then proceeds to more specifically connect homophobia to other forms of nazi domination and questions the wisdom of received scholarship that reduces nazi fascism to a symptom of homosexuality. Finally, I examine the possible connections of nazi homophobia, and its imbrication with other deployments of power, for the study of contemporary culture, in which the homophobic impulse continues to reverberate and calls into question readings of history steeped in linear notions of progressive modernity. The book concludes with an exploration of some of its implications for thinking about the ongoing social, cultural, and historical significance of the Holocaust in new ways in a twenty-first century world.

The book begins by situating sexuality, as an axis of theoretical investigation, further into historical work on the Third Reich and into Holocaust scholarship since nazi racial politics were inscribed politically into the rewriting of the German nation and into the social construction of those marked as social outsiders. A corollary argument made in chapter 1 is that nazi homophobia and accompanying anxieties of social and sexual degeneracy within the nation help elaborate understandings of nazi anti-Semitism and nazi racial politics. In the specific context of Holocaust scholarship, the Jewish/non-Jewish split that often structures understandings of nazi victims in received scholarship requires deconstruction. This is necessary not to delegitimate the Judaic significance of the Holocaust, but to move outside of the very dualism which informed every aspect of nazi social policy. It also helps to open up new lines of inquiry and allow for more careful examination of the interimplications of nazi power across the social register, so that broader understandings of nazi genocide can be developed in future work. This implies moving away from an understanding of nazi homophobia as a single vector of power, which would foreclose the ways in which homophobia was deeply embedded in German nationalism, racial hygiene, and eugenics, since it is important to understand the ways in which homosexuality signified as part of larger discursive and ideological practices within National Socialism. The chapter also acknowledges the important precedent of work on gender, which I alluded to at the beginning of this introduction, as gender studies has helped challenge the predominance of the male gaze in Holocaust scholarship (and in history more generally). This book takes that assumption further by theorizing that gaze not only as masculine but as heteronormative. Finally, drawing from Hannah Arendt's *The Origins of Totalitarianism*, the first chapter asks how postcolonial frameworks for understanding imperialism might be helpful in rereading Europe and totalitarian rule in the decline and aftermath of imperialism, not only in terms of the construction of a self-ordained master race within a self-proclaimed superior culture, but in terms of what this implies for the politics of sexual difference in both racist regimes of European imperialism and later totalitarianism (especially German fascism).

Developing further a Foucauldian framework to situate homosexuality within signifying practices under the Third Reich, chapter 2 argues against simplistic schemes that depict homosexual victims as persecuted for "what they did." The chapter examines specific instantiations of nazi juridical law, substantiated by historical documents, that situate homosexuality in the public sphere and as always already socially mediated and culturally constructed rather than only being intimately felt and practiced, and rather than being confined merely to the peripheries of the social field. The specific extension of Paragraph 175 of the Reich Penal Code in 1935 and the establishment of the Reichszentrale zur Bekämpfung der Homosexualität und der Abtreibung (Central Reich Office for the Combating of Homosexuality and Abortion) in 1936 shifted the prosecution of "unnatural sex acts" (sodomy) to sexual offenses that could include, under the sign of homosexuality, kissing, embracing, fondling between men, and fantasies and expressions of desire in private letters or in personal conversation. This helped to increase the persecution of homosexuals, since it was assumed that they would use their sexuality as a weapon against society as did Jews, and both Jews and homosexuals were marked by sexual excess and effeminacy in the nazi propaganda deployed against them. This racialization of sexuality, buttressed by its medicalization in late nineteenth-century medical literature (which read both homosexuals and Jews in terms of feminine body movements, proneness to hysteria, and as degenerates who violated accepted modes of social respectability and gender conformity), was further evident, I argue, in the setting up of the Reichszentrale Office by a special directive from Himmler. My contention is that the nazis needed to ensure not only that the sovereignty and purity of the Aryan race was protected, but that the German birth rate flourished. The bureaucratic conscription of homosexuals, especially those who were deemed to be "opportunistic," rather than congenital, and could be "re-educated" to perform their reproductive duties to preserve and ensure the status and respectability of the Nordic race and the strength of the German state, was very much tied to nazi population policy.

On the basis of the argument made in chapter 2 that the nazis coded homosexuality as a Semitic invention under tropes of waywardness and excess, chapter 3 turns to the specificity of lesbian existence under the Third Reich and attempts to challenge prevailing assumptions in Holocaust scholarship that lesbians were not as systematically persecuted simply because lesbian sex was not specifically criminalized in Paragraph 175. When the axis of gender does not exceed or completely override the axis of sexuality, which otherwise reduces same-sex desire to gay men or to cross-gender identified lesbians, and when one looks beyond the confines of the pink triangle used to mark gay male prisoners in concentration camps, it becomes possible for a lesbian narrative space, within the domain of Holocaust research, to emerge. I argue that though the lesbian subcultures that flourished in German cities under the Weimar set an important cultural and historical precedent that did not eradicate completely all forms of lesbian existence under the Third Reich precisely because lesbian sex was not criminalized, many lesbian testimonials reveal affectional and erotic bonds between women under the Third Reich in Germany and also in France, especially after the German occupation. Such testimonials also reveal that lesbian experiences of displacement, forced migration, and separation from lovers engendered fears of *possible* persecution under National Socialism alongside actual prosecutions and deportations. But the mere fact that lesbians were not specifically criminalized by the nazis does not imply that it was not dangerous to be lesbian. Indeed, some nazi jurists and social critics argued vehemently for the inclusion of the erotic bonds between women in the criminal code on the grounds that any type of women's emancipation and erotic autonomy were a threat to marriage and the family and undermined prevailing social structures and social norms. It is important to note that these debates were ongoing and that the final decision not to prosecute lesbians under Paragraph 175 was not handed down until 1942 from the Reich Minister of Justice. So during most of the nazi era, lesbians could have been subjected, as many were, to persecution, physical and sexual harassment, rape, and detention in camps. As with the case of gay men, references to nazi population policy informed the surveillance of sexuality. For example, a nazi conduct book written for Aryan women interpreted masculinization in women as a sign of a degenerate foreign race, since "healthy races do not artificially blur the differences between the sexes."[4] Many women were labeled as "asocial" and persecuted for their resistance to fixed gender norms centering on marriage, procreation, and restriction to the domestic sphere; in addition, many were punished for their resistance to the sexual advances by nazi officers with whom they had worked or come into close contact. And many such women were lesbian.

While some research, especially informed by psychoanalysis, has read nazi hypermasculinity as a struggle for the repudiation of femininity and as a yearning for male comradeship that occurred in the trenches and at battle during World War I, and earlier in a tradition that celebrated the sharing of male physical strength in the German *Männerbund* (which often included passionate, and possibly erotic, bonds between men), chapter 4 attempts a re-analysis of the problematic reduction of nazi fascism to a repression of femininity and therefore of latent homosexuality. Such a perspective converts homosexuals from the status of victims of nazi power (barely recognized as such in the postwar years and long afterward) and potentially puts them on a par with nazi perpetrators and thereby, as Andrew Hewitt remarks, risks "hypostatizing homosexuality as absolutely external to the subject of homophobic social and political discourse" (*Political Inversions* 11). Such a conflation of political with sexual deviance—what Hewitt refers to as a kind of "homofascism"—is also evident in theories of fascism articulated by Theodor Adorno and others of the Frankfurt School. Moreover, I argue that the rendering of nazi fascists as sexually flawed and gender dysphoric vilifies homosexuality in ways similar to the nazi vilification not only of homosexuals, but of other groups, such as Jews, in sexually deviant terms. Such approaches elide the ways in which homosexuality operated discursively within larger systems of signifying practices under National Socialism, and do not take homosexuality out of particular bodies so that it can be situated socially, historically, and discursively. In using psychoanalysis as a lens with which to view queer fascism, evident in Klaus Theweleit's work on the *Freikorps*, for example, it is similarly important to queer psychoanalytic thinking and expose its blind spots to the extent that it molds fascist identities to its grid of inscription and intelligibility through creating a causal link between fascism and homosexuality, while keeping cultural hegemonies pertaining to gender and sexuality in place. The chapter concludes by asking the extent to which the relegation of fascism to the exclusive domain of men is a historical contingency or an inherent trait, while acknowledging that it may be reassuring for feminists to think of fascism as a problem of phallic masculinity. The chapter similarly points to the reductive conflation of sexual identity with political affiliation, given the attraction to fascist politics by socially prominent lesbians (and gay men) in Europe in the interwar years as a way of restoring a stable social order in the years following World War I. This was tied to their allegiance to the values and economic privileges of their social class, and to their fear of a competing ideology—communism—and is a rather harsh reminder that a causal link between liberal politics and sexual alterity has not always been the case historically. Moreover, this history is a subtle reminder, particularly in the context of this and related studies, to avoid sentimentalizing a queer past.

Rather than reading nazi homophobia as a momentary aberration limited to a specific, isolated moment in history, chapter 5, through the analysis of a range of signifying practices, explores discursive traces of the ongoing markings of sexual dissidents as social outsiders during the postwar years and in contemporary culture. While acknowledging the continued criminalization of homosexuality in the Federal Republic of Germany through Paragraph 175 (which remained in the penal code until 1969 and was an impediment for homosexuals to be recognized as victims of the nazi atrocities committed against them), the chapter also points out that during the postwar period, psychiatry and psychoanalysis reached their homophobic height following the publication of the Kinsey Report in 1948. (This was particularly the case in the United States, although the international ramifications were substantial.) The Kinsey Report incited studies on the etiology of homosexuality by Irving Bieber and others, studies that sought to back up the social pathologization of homosexuality with clinical evidence. The publication of the first and second editions of the *Diagnostic and Statistical Manual of Mental Disorders* (*DSM-I* and *II*) by the American Psychiatric Association (APA) in 1952 and 1968, respectively, listed homosexuality as a diagnostic category, initially as sociopathic (in the *DSM-I*) and later as psychopathological and as a learned rebellion to existing cultural and social norms (in the *DSM-II*). What this short history reveals is an attempt not only to make homosexuality more culturally legible within the paranoia and uncertainty of the Cold War era, but to manage it medically and socially within the postwar economic boom fueled by consumption geared toward the conventional heterosexual family. While not fervently tied to racial politics, as was the case under the Third Reich, the medical, and therefore social, discursive, and cultural management of homosexuality, through the conflation of psychological health with social/sexual conformity, was not completely dissimilar to the Third Reich's social and medical management of sexual otherness.

Yet more specific ties to the politics of race are evident, the chapter argues, in the initial phases of the HIV/AIDS pandemic under tropes of perversion, sexual indulgence, and moral laxity for those infected to the extent that the virus in the early to mid-1980s was thought to be limited to gay men and intravenous drug users. Yet the cutting back of federal funding for drug and poverty programs in the United States under the Reagan administration in the 1980s simultaneously cut back needed funds to manage effectively the ensuing HIV/AIDS crisis. Poor racial minorities and those in socially vulnerable groups were left without protection or resources to face the impact of AIDS. Further, with increasing rates of infection in Africa, the pandemic gained social meaning through traditional, deep-seated prejudices regarding race, class, gender, and sexuality. The global management of AIDS, which initially read African sexuality as licentious and primitive when the human immunodeficiency virus was transmitted heterosexually, was slanted accordingly. The further racialization of sexuality in the postcolonial world is analyzed in instances where homosexuality is regarded in nationalist imaginaries as a western aberration, alien to indigenous cultural traditions. The chapter ends by pointing to the continued denial of rights to gay men, lesbians, and the transgendered in many parts of the world today, especially true in the case of women, where lesbians are often prone to more severe punishment by torture, rape, prison, and in some cases, death. While not specifically reducible to genocide or to the nazi pogrom against homosexuals (though quite close in terms of its discursive and cultural significance), continued indifference to the social stigmatization of sexual otherness in the name of home, family, or national or cultural sovereignty frequently justifies various legal forms of psychic or physical violence against lesbians, gay men, and the transgendered and denies them close emotional bonds and erotic autonomy as viable human rights.

In recognizing the uniqueness of the Holocaust as a historical event, the final chapter speaks to the Holocaust's ongoing significance when it is subjected to a range of pressing social, cultural, and political questions. The framing of new questions has helped to open up sexuality as an important lens of inquiry not only in terms of making specific sexual identities more legible, but by showing how struggles over sexuality and erotic autonomy are always already inflected with other relations of power. Moreover, by neglecting sexuality and an analysis of sexual alterity in Holocaust studies, one obfuscates how political institutions, juridical and bureaucratic systems, and the social production of knowledge by dominant groups affect individual lives in the broadest possible sense, which would be detrimental to understanding the ongoing impact of the Holocaust in the contemporary world. Similarly, the chapter argues for "queer" as a lens and intellectual perspective with which to read against the grain of heterotextual narrative in Holocaust research so as to locate alternative pathways of meaning. Such pathways, I must argue, do not contaminate the "purity" of the Holocaust, which recalls nazi tropes and obsessions about racial purity, but demand self-reflexive, and often sobering, attention to the often socially biased ways in which history is narrated and knowledge is produced. An ongoing theorization of the Holocaust and its continued significance, alongside queer theory as a hermeneutic tool, can form an important conjunction of interdisciplinary inquiry in order to analyze where various forms of power intersect in history and culture. At the same time, such a theorization can generate important new thinking on the meaning of social justice and human rights in the twenty-first century. This book by no means attempts to situate queer theory as a new kind of master discourse with which to read the Holocaust, nor does it attempt to tip-toe around Holocaust studies so as not to offend more established lines of inquiry. Far from any grandiose claims, the present work only hopes that the meaningful conjunction of Holocaust and queer studies will help unfold lines of inquiry that remain to be taken up and further explored.

1

Holocaust Studies Meets Queer Studies: A Contested Alliance?

Why write a book on the positions of lesbians and gay men under National Socialism? Certainly historical work on the period traditionally has not paid serious attention to this topic until relatively recently. Beginning in the 1980s and 1990s, several memoirs by gay men and lesbians who survived nazi persecution in its various forms were published, though this work has been primarily confined to gay men.[1] Looking at the Holocaust through another lens and more explicitly theorizing the politics of sexuality under nazism may help point to blind spots or gaps in thinking based on a long absence of the interrogation of state-sponsored homophobia as a significant vector of nazi power. It may also enable new ways of reading and understanding the atrocities of nazi rule, including the Holocaust. This does not, of course, imply that all forms of nazi oppression can be reduced to sameness, but recognizes that they were differentially structured and that homophobia operated in collaboration with other vectors of nazi power, which can shed light on distinctive nodes of social and cultural organization both in the nazi era and in the present.

It is also important to understand the significance of the Holocaust more broadly by challenging some prevailing views that regard homosexuality as unthinkable for Holocaust research, and to question the Jewish/non-Jewish opposition with respect to Holocaust victims. It cannot be denied, as Carol Rittner observes, that the Holocaust was a deliberate attempt by Hitler and the nazis, over a twelve-year period, to annihilate systematically European Jews and to eradicate all traces of Jewish religious and cultural life in Europe. Yet, at the same time, the historical record indicates that not all victims were Jews (xi–xii). Other victims included Roma, Sinti, Jehovah Witnesses,

Slavs, Poles, the mentally and physically handicapped, homosexuals, political prisoners, criminals, and resistant women, a significant number of whom were lesbian, as I shall discuss in chapter 3. Historically, since the Holocaust became a topic of academic research in the early 1960s, and since the subsequent inception of Holocaust studies as a discipline in the 1970s,[2] there has been a divide in terms of understanding Jews as the primary victims of nazi policies across the social register, and an attempt to understand other victims of nazi persecution who also suffered and were murdered. As Michael Berenbaum succinctly frames the issue, there is the position articulated by Elie Wiesel that acknowledges that while not all victims of nazi atrocities were Jews, all Jews were victims by virtue of being Jewish, and that a focus on other victims may detract from the Judaic specificity of the Holocaust and the systematic murder of seven million Jews and the effacement of their memory. The other position, articulated by Simon Wiesenthal, maintains that the Holocaust transcended the confines of the Jewish community and that there were other victims (Berenbaum, "The Uniqueness and Universality of the Holocaust" 20–22). In writing this book, I accept and understand the Judaic significance of the Holocaust, in that no other group was persecuted and murdered so systematically and relentlessly as a matter of state policy and in the name of the maintenance of white racial purity and superiority. Yet a larger assumption of this study is that an understanding of other victims of the nazis will deepen our understanding of the Holocaust and of nazi fascism to the extent that nazi racial politics were indeed present in the persecution of other social groups, as was the case with their persecution of gay men and lesbians.

On one level, the specificity of Jewish experiences of the Holocaust can actually be deepened as they are refracted through the marking and persecution of other social groups as outsiders, while other vectors of nazi power, such as homophobia and fears of social and sexual degeneracy, can shed further light on nazi anti-Semitism and racism. Not only is the Jewish/non-Jewish split in Holocaust studies intellectually limiting to the extent that it forecloses discussion of the interimplications of various vectors of nazi power, such as those pertaining to race and sexuality, it is also historically limiting insofar as it maintains the division between Jews and Gentiles, a division maintained by the ideology of nazism. The split is also politically limiting, given that it confers status and problematic hierarchies among the various victims. The interimplications of various vectors of nazi power do not imply, I must reiterate, that all forms of nazi power were congruent or that all groups who were persecuted had identical experiences. But challenging the Jewish/non-Jewish opposition helps to open up new lines of inquiry and enables a broader theorization of nazi genocide and its discursive traces and potential seedlings in the contemporary world. It is for these reasons that I accept Berenbaum's important stipulation that there is no conflict between describing the uniqueness of Jewish experiences under the Holocaust and the inclusion of other victims of nazism ("The Uniqueness and Universality of the Holocaust" 32). This book, then, is one attempt at that inclusion through a more rigorous theorization of the positions of gay men and lesbians not through a mere exposure of homophobia as a singular and separate vector of nazi domination, but by an analysis of homosexuality under the Third Reich as implicated in German nationalism, population and racial politics, and anxieties about the threat of social degeneracy.

At the same time, nazi representations, debates, policies, and persecutions inscribed in social discourses surrounding homosexuality were not singular, separate aberrations with consequences only for homosexuals. They were part of a much larger strategy of social disenfranchisement and the marking of "enemies" of the state—the devaluation of those who were different, particularly Jews, stretching to other social groups as well who were thought to undermine Aryan racial purity. Further, not only does the interimplication of nazi homophobia with other forms of domination pertaining to race, gender, religion, political creed, and physical and mental health reveal distinctive nodes of social and cultural organization under the Third Reich, as I have already mentioned, but has contemporary implications and consequences when benefits and protections are denied to those marked as sexually other through the redeployment of similar strategies of exclusion.[3]

An important precedent for enabling different cultural interpretations of the Holocaust in the nazi period has been work on gender analysis. This work, as Sara Horowitz observes, has helped exemplify the marginality of women's experiences within the master narratives of nazi genocide. This is particularly true in that, in many memoirs, whatever women have experienced separately from men is often regarded as superfluous, or as reducible to men's experiences, and is therefore often lost as memory or testimony (111), given the primacy of the male gaze in most Holocaust scholarship. Yet gender is a crucial lens of inquiry and analysis not only to understand better the general oppression of women under the Third Reich (and the differences between the oppression of German women and that of Jewish, Roma, Sinti, and Slavic women, for example), but also to understand heteronormativity as a regime that imposes a stringent policing of gender norms and maintains them as fixed as part of the overall project of protecting Aryan racial purity. Moreover, gender is a highly salient site for analyzing the relationship between homosexuality and the Holocaust. While gender and sexuality are interrelated axes of analysis—with the stipulation that one is not reducible to the other—an analysis of gender enables a better understanding of the specific positions of lesbians under the Third Reich. It also allows us to consider further the relation between women and fascism against traditional approaches that read fascism strictly as the domain of men with latent or repressed homosexual desires. These two important points will be discussed more specifically in chapters 3 and 4 respectively. At the same time, Horowitz's argument is that work on gender can produce a wider variety of contexts in which the Holocaust took place and perhaps even widen the parameters of what is remembered (116). The same is true for an analysis of sexuality, particularly since it does not approach the Holocaust, and the historical period preceding and surrounding it, from a universalist or so-called neutral frame of reference since this would obscure the fact that any approach is always already political and would fail to engage or challenge the primacy of the (hetero-)masculinist gaze that has traditionally been the authoritative narrative voice of Holocaust scholarship.

This book attempts to situate homosexuality socially and historically rather than locating it in the body or in particular identities alone.[4] It challenges the rendering of homosexuals as victims of the Holocaust in the research based solely on *what they did*, as such a distinction problematically reduces sexuality to articulated and enacted desires alone, a problem the nazis themselves recognized in their revision of Paragraph 175 of the Reich Penal Code.[5] Initial work on homosexuality that I mentioned at the beginning of this chapter often focused on the testimonials of specific individuals and the persecution they suffered as a result of their sexuality. Other work sought to reproduce documents and texts attesting to the persecution of homosexuals as a matter of historical record. However, while memory and the recuperation of historical data that speak to the persecution of gay men and lesbians are important to providing recognition of homosexuals as victims of nazi power—a political act in and of itself, considering the plight of many homosexuals after the war and the historical elisions in Holocaust scholarship—these approaches do not go far enough to situate homosexuality as part of a larger system of social and cultural organization and to account for its historical specificity. As I have thus far argued, it is important not to limit (homo)sexuality to a singular axis of analysis, that is, not to read it as merely a given. Rather, it is helpful to situate it *relationally*, so as to enable it to appear, as David Halperin reminds us, as one of many documented varieties and effects of human social organization (22–23), as was certainly the case within the larger context of National Socialist policy.

This book takes a Foucauldian approach to understanding the positions of sexual dissidents by situating sexuality within discursive and institutional practices, reading sexuality as a site of cultural production within the nazi period, and accounting for the ways in which it signified under specific sets of historical, material, and ideological conditions that were part of a wider range of discursive practices pertaining to racial hygiene, eugenics, nazi fears of social degeneracy, and other nationalist goals. By institutional practices, I mean laws, apparatuses of social surveillance and detection, and other social structures (re)shaped by the production of discourses on sexuality under National Socialism—and even previously under the Weimar, as I discuss in chapter 2. In *The History of Sexuality*, Foucault speaks of how sexuality forms a vast discursive network as a means of reading and interpreting culture. He writes:

> Sexuality must not be thought of as a kind of natural given which power tries to hold in check, or as an obscure domain which knowledge tries gradually to uncover. It is the name that can be given to a historical construct: not a furtive reality that is difficult to grasp, but a great surface network in which the stimulation of bodies, the intensification of pleasures, the incitement to discourse, the formation of special knowledges, the strengthening of controls and resistances, are linked to one another, in accordance with a few major strategies of knowledge and power. (105–6)

Foucault's approach does not allow us to fetishize homosexuality as a single axis of difference under National Socialism or in any other particular historical period or social context. It demands instead that it be situated within broader signifying systems in culture. Yet while homosexuality sits at the nexus of a range of social discourses, both within National Socialism and within the specific domain of Holocaust scholarship, it is still very important not to lose sight of the specificity of homosexuality and to be careful not to render it invisible in nazi social practices, since this has been precisely its legacy in research and scholarship on the period. This book is one attempt, through its title, topic, and approach, to theorize more deeply the historic record and perhaps takes it a bit further—a delicate balancing act—without essentializing gay or lesbian identity. In addition, it intends to be careful not to assume erroneously that homophobia operated as a separate vector of nazi power, unencumbered by the vast network of signifying practices surrounding German nationhood under the Third Reich. Queer theory, with its endless proliferation of social differences, resists normativities pertaining to race, gender, class, national fantasy, the family, and other social norms, categories, and institutions *in addition to* sexuality. This implies not only a challenge to identic fixity, whereby sexual identity is regarded as "uninflected by the pressures of other subjectivizing factors" (Harper 26), but an unhinging of "queer" from gender and sexuality alone by looking at the ways in which race, ethnicity, and other subject positions also inflect sexuality so that all fixities and normativities are always already displaced, deferred, ruptured. In the context of Holocaust studies, this does not render particular groups of victims invisible, nor does it dilute the effects of nazi power on other social groups. Instead it recognizes that one cannot talk about racial or anti-Semitic oppression without considering sexuality and gender, national affiliation, social class, religion, and other aspects of subjective identification, and without recognizing that nazi domination operated along several vectors of oppression simultaneously in its persecution of any one social group. This is an important point, as I do not wish to assume that Foucault provides an unproblematic tool for better understanding the positions of gay men and lesbians under the Third Reich. The production of discourses pertaining to the medical pathologization of homosexuality in the nineteenth century elides the similarities, as I have pointed out elsewhere, to imperial constructions of racial otherness which were conflated with deviant sexuality in the colonies, and which justified the need for colonial control. Yet this specific racialization of sexuality, that is, the interimplication of race and sexuality under imperial rule, is elided in Foucault's history of sexuality.[6]

When Foucault says sexuality is a historical construct rather than a furtive reality that would not shift over time and across space, and that sexuality is not merely a biological or psychological phenomenon, this means that sexuality is discursively, and therefore socially, situated. When Foucault mentions in *The History of Sexuality* the famous shift in nineteenth-century discourses from understanding homosexuality as a specific act (of sodomy) to a particular identity,[7] the shift is *discursive* and a significant historical marker to which Halperin refers as the internal logic and systematic function of two different styles of sexual disqualification (32). I am interested in how nazi policies systematically disqualified sexual subjects, as these strategies of national disbelonging were connected to the wider range of nazi policies on racial hygiene, social degeneracy, and eugenics. That is, I am interested in how these helped to form part of the threads that constructed the fabric of German nationalism under the Third Reich. I will discuss not only the transversal of sexuality by other vectors of power under nazism, but the ways in which discourses on sexuality were set within nazi formulations of Aryan racial superiority and German statehood and empire. I will also consider the ways in which homosexuality, as connected intimately to these policies, incited institutionally articulated discourses and social practices of regulation, discipline, and surveillance. When Foucault talks about sexuality as discursive, then, he does not mean that sexuality itself is merely a discourse since it can also be about the intensification of pleasures and the stimulation of bodies. Yet, more than being a private, intimate act alone, sexuality is also a political category entwined and interfused with social meaning. It is also located at the nexus of a range of heterogeneous discourses and institutional practices that have arisen out of specific historical, ideological, and material conditions as they obviously did within the parameters of the nazi state.

But research on homosexuality under the Third Reich, especially when it is addressed within the domain of Holocaust scholarship, has until very recently occurred separately in an understandable and politically justified effort to address gay men and lesbians as victims of nazi power.[8] This book does not attempt to undermine that important work, which is still ongoing, given a historical reluctance in dominant Holocaust scholarship to engage sexual difference critically as a category of analysis, given the continued pathologization of homosexuality as symptomatic of fascist desire in the elite corps of male nazi leaders in other work, and given a predominant (straight) male gaze and narrative point of view in research that does not go far enough to interrogate heteronormativity not only as a strategy of power under National Socialism, but as an unchallenged assumption in research and knowledge production in Holocaust studies. An approach that accounts for Foucauldian understandings of sexuality allows for a more fluid and explicit theorization of the politics of sexuality under nazism. More important, it allows sexuality to emerge as a more salient lens of inquiry in the nazi period without narrowly singling it out as a completely separate category of analysis apart from the materialities of historical and cultural processes. At the same time, it is important to note, as I hope to show in this book, that while homosexuality was relegated to the margins of national belonging under National Socialism, it was very much central to nazi racial and social policy.

But while the specificity of historical difference is important, I also wish to show that the alterities of/in the past, and the ways in which (homo)sexuality may provide a useful lens to make visible a viable node of social and cultural organization for understanding the nazi period, need not be confined to the past alone. In fact, similar—though not reducible—nodes of social organization and existence may also be exposed as operating since the nazi period and in the present day, though recast in slightly different, shifting terms. As Halperin notes, respecting historical alterity need not preclude present continuities (17). With this in mind, how is sexuality, as a significant marker of social organization under the Third Reich, differentially redeployed in the postwar period, during the Cold War, in postcolonial strategies of decolonization, and in the HIV/AIDS pandemic? What have we really learned about nazi atrocities? Can they merely be relegated to the past, and have we necessarily become more enlightened, less violent and barbaric, by virtue of simply having come further along in time?

There is another impetus for this book beyond the mere recovery of gay and lesbian lives through considering sexuality as a discursive production under nazism and as a significant marker of social organization. In a recently completed study of the politics of sexual difference in post-apartheid South Africa, I acknowledged the imperial and apartheid legacies that preceded the transition to full democracy and the reverberating effects of this in the region. Now I attempt to understand the ways in which postcolonial frameworks for understanding imperialism, nationhood, and citizenship might be useful in (re)reading Europe, the former center of territorial colonialism and continued economic imperialism. How might we better understand totalitarian rule in the aftermath of the height of European imperialism, particularly using sexuality as one (but not the only) marker of social and cultural organization? How might sexuality further elaborate racial politics under National Socialism, as it did under apartheid and its aftermath in continued struggles for full democracy in South Africa, with the stipulation, of course, that one regime is not reducible to the other?

After completing *Imperialism within the Margins*, I was rather struck by Hannah Arendt's point in *The Origins of Totalitarianism* that it is no longer possible to isolate anti-Semitic ideology from issues that are thought to be completely unrelated to the realities of modern Jewish history (xvi). Though Arendt may not have had the politics of sexuality specifically in mind, she does acknowledge the importance of examining other lines of inquiry that may not be specific to Jewish history. I would add, however, that homosexuals who were Jewish were most certainly victims of anti-Semitic ideology, as were homosexuals in general to the extent that sexuality was always already racialized under nazi power. What Arendt does, however, is to help broaden received notions of anti-Semitism without in any way trivializing Judaic experiences of anti-Semitism before, during, and after National Socialism or without undermining specific Jewish experiences of the Holocaust. More strikingly, Arendt notices a link between imperialism and its gradual decline in the years leading up to World War I and the various forms of totalitarianism that arose simultaneously in Europe at the time. Speaking of the period 1884–1914, both the height and beginning of the decline of imperialism, Arendt writes: "Some of the fundamental aspects of this time appear so close to totalitarian phenomena of the twentieth century that it may be justifiable to consider the whole period a preparatory stage for coming catastrophes" (123). For Arendt, imperialism reached its apex as a result of the incongruity between the nation-state system, which defined nations within discrete borders and specific geographical locations, and the result of rapid economic and industrial development in Europe in the last part of the nineteenth century. The latter enabled the nation-states of the imperialist colonizers, such as Britain, France, Spain, Holland, Italy, and Portugal, to extend their national borders, monopolize trade routes, and widen their political and economic influence in the world. Arendt proposes a link between the expansionism of European colonialism and nazi totalitarianism to the extent that, similar to their colonial predecessors, the nazis saw themselves as belonging to a master race self-evidently endowed and qualified to rule over what they considered to be inferior races at home and abroad (206). While Arendt locates India as the center of colonial wealth and marks the decline of imperialism in the voluntary liquidation of British rule in India—which then made it difficult for European nations to maintain their hold on their overseas possessions (xvii)—her assertion calls into question the mere displacement of the proliferation of modern nationalisms in Europe in the eighteenth and nineteenth centuries to the colonies where such understandings of the nation did not emerge historically. The nationalist imaginaries that developed out of the process of decolonization during and after colonial rule were not mere products of European nationalism, since those that developed in the postcolonial world did not emerge out of the political and social history of western Europe. This implies, then, a slightly different understanding of postcolonial nationalisms, since their specific history and materiality must be taken into account, a point to which I shall return shortly.

The postcolonial nationalisms that developed initially under imperial rule and then after independence do enable important rereadings of Europe, particularly of National Socialism. Imperialism made visible the expansion of national power beyond the discrete borders of the nation-state and brought about the imagined possibility, indeed the fantasy, of global domination, a project that was redeployed under slightly different terms in nazi expansionism and goals for eventual global power. Imperialism and its attendant notions of racial superiority helped stamp the mark of "backwardness" or primitivity onto non-European cultures, which served as the justification for imperialism's civilizing mission. This was the case particularly in Africa, where strict racial boundaries and a sense of cultural superiority were essential, as Barbara Bush argues, to legitimizing colonial rule and the racial order that sustained it (8). In my own research on South Africa, I argued that though apartheid was legislated in 1948, the social and political conditions for it were put into place in the years following the Anglo-Boer War of 1899–1902 in a series of Native Land Acts that kept indigenous Africans apart from British and Afrikaner whites (*Imperialism within the Margins* 83–85). Both regimes of imperialism and apartheid in South Africa and National Socialism in Germany used race as a ruling device and as a way of bolstering white European (or Aryan in the case of National Socialism) superiority.

While I do not have the space here for a more detailed comparison of European imperialism (and its effects in South Africa) with German fascism, or for a comparison of the use of race in imperialism and apartheid in South Africa with nazism in Germany in terms of how a new body politic was set up in order to relegate particular groups to the margins of society and replace entire systems of culture thought to be inferior (though the nazis notably took this much further than ghettoization and the stripping of property and fundamental human rights from those subjected to their power), I am interested in the ways in which sexuality was interimplicated in the social and political fabric of such regimes. In *Imperialism within the Margins,* I argued that the politics of sexuality in the "new" South Africa could not be understood apart from post-apartheid politics, nor could South African sexual politics be understood apart from the historical antecedent of colonialism and apartheid as homophobia was encoded into both racist regimes. Keeping this framework in mind, though adjusting the interrogatory optic slightly to adjust to a different social and historical context in Europe, I acknowledge National Socialism in this book as an anti-Semitic and racist regime but not without the intersectionality of homophobia and gender oppression, as these—and other vectors of nazi power—were connected to broader goals of eugenics, population politics, and the maintenance of Aryan purity. The racialization of sexuality, as I argue in chapter 2, enabled the further encoding of homophobia into juridical law (through the revision of Paragraph 175 of the Reich Penal Code) and into institutional practices. The transformation was similar to the ways in which imperialism justified the disciplining of indigenous bodies in southern Africa based on racist readings of African (homo)sexuality as decadent, repulsive, and punishable by law.[9]

There is a connection between imperialism and nazi totalitarianism through desires for global expansion (an idea unthinkable in the West prior to the beginnings of colonialism in the seventeenth century), the marking of non-European, non-western cultures as inferior, and notions of white racial supremacy encoded into juridical law, all of which have sexual meanings and connotations. Yet there is also a link to twentieth-century European totalitarianisms from the other side of the imperial equation to the extent that postcolonial nationalisms, in the aftermath of colonial rule, have also made use of and have enacted strategies of social exclusion that mark certain groups on the constitutive outside of new nationhood and national belonging in the present day. Postcolonial theory has pointed out quite convincingly that postcolonial nation-states evolved out of a different set of historical and cultural conditions not centered around European ideals of wealth, industriousness, progress, and liberal democracy alone, though they have been influenced by these, because the crucial historical difference in the configuration of the postcolonial nation-state's narrative of itself is the historical materiality of colonialism and its ongoing effects. For this reason, as postcolonial theorists such as Partha Chatterjee have argued, postcolonial nationalism is often bifurcated; that is, it is a search for the regeneration of national culture to reach the standards of progress and development set by an alien (western) culture, and simultaneously a rejection of alien (colonial and later western) influences that impinge upon and threaten the distinctive spiritual aspects of national culture (*Nationalist Thought* 2). In other words, postcolonial nationalism is part of an ideological struggle to make the nation sovereign, which, different from its European counterpart, begins at the time the state is in the hands of a western colonial power (Chatterjee, *Nation and Its Fragments* 6), and is not reducible only to the period leading up to and following independence from colonial rule.

More audible struggles in the processes of decolonization leading up to World War II, and the decline of empire and its aftermath, engendered a further articulation of nationalist goals in many of the colonies as they transitioned to independence; additionally these articulations have continued after independence as a mode of opposition to the history of colonial rule. The process of decolonization, the effects of which remain today, was, and continues to be, an attempt to shake off the last vestiges of imperialism by asserting the importance of national culture, national languages, and indigenous culture and history insofar as these were suppressed under colonialism. At the same time, however, as I have argued previously, in the case of southern Africa, postcolonial nationalism often slides from a mode of opposition (to colonial rule) to a mode of oppression as new forms of national belonging and the assertion of indigenous cultural heritage create new social hierarchies and strategies of social exclusion. National regeneration, in the name of a new national identity, operates by defining what is "alien" to national culture in a similar way that the denotation or meaning of any term in language is dependent on what is exterior to it—the master trope of signification from the perspective of Saussurean linguistics, where language is thought to function as a system of relations and differences.

While the specific historical and social contexts of the development of particular postcolonial narratives of nationhood are different and cannot be reduced to sameness, similar tropes and rhetorical strategies of interior/exterior, inside/outside, center/margin operated under National Socialism. Interestingly, they continue to do so under postcolonial cultural nationalisms, both of which have cast homosexuality as exterior to national culture. In the former case, homosexuality was racialized because it was thought to contradict Third Reich goals of eugenics and population growth among Aryans and was conflated with weakness. Homosexuals, like Jews, were assumed to use their sexuality to weaken the nation. And in the latter case of postcolonial nationalisms, homosexuality continues to be racialized as a remnant of empire, as a white western decadence, and therefore as foreign to indigenous cultures.[10] Rather than repeating the imperialist gesture that attempts to read the postcolonial world through a European cultural history, I am wondering if it might be possible to read National Socialism and its strategies of social exclusion, especially of gay men and lesbians, partly through the lens and influence of postcolonial formations of the nation, as a sort of reversal, whereby the former colonies—and scholarship taking place within or about them—speak back to and frame the European imperial center, in this case nazi Germany, as an object of analysis and critique.[11] Such an approach also enables a critique of linear, progressive views of history, given that European imperialism, including the imperialism of the Third Reich, was based on racial superiority and a racialization of homosexuality, which articulated Europe as the center (specifically Germany in the case of National Socialism), and the rest of the world as its periphery. Reformulated racializations of homosexuality, in the professed attempt to decolonize and assert the difference of indigenous cultures, have continued under very different conditions in postcolonial contexts in the present day, yet maintain a very similar inside/outside, center/periphery dichotomy within the postcolonial nation-state. This is not to reduce postcolonial nationalisms in any way to National Socialism; it is only to point critically to the links of (homo)sexuality as a site of weakness or regression in rearticulations of the nation-state as a way of restoring its power following its traumatic loss, through the effects of imperial rule in postcolonial contexts, and through the political and economic effects of the loss of World War I in Germany.

If totalitarianism, in the form of nazi fascism, represents a return of imperialism to Europe in a new guise—that is, a racist regime in a new key, built on ideas of global and economic hegemony but not without its sexual component—and if there is a link to the rendering of gay men and lesbians to the constitutive outside of national belonging as inscribed in established and emerging nationalist discourses in the postcolonies to the extent that homosexuality is deployed as a dangerous impediment to indigenous cultural purity and national cohesion, then it is important that homosexuality, and all forms of sexual dissidence, be studied not in terms of erotic practices or social identities alone that threaten heteroerotic social organization, but as legible cultural signifiers to be studied and analyzed within the larger discursive network of signifying practices that comprise culture.

What ultimately threatens to tear the fantasized shorn-up fabrics of imperialism, nationalism, or totalitarianism is not lesbians or gay men per se, but the specter of gender deviance, male passivity, and ultimately the fear of the weakening of the nation-state and its imperial desires through the ideological penetration of homosexuality as the signifier which cannot be contained. It is the circulation of homosexuality under regimes of power (such as European imperialism, nazi fascism, postcolonial nationalism) and its challenges to gender, racial, class, sexual, and other social normativities that point to and extend the ambivalence of those sites of power. The ultimate threat of homosexuality is not particular identities or sexual practices alone, but the threat of the feminization of the nation-state, always imagined as masculine, and it is this, along with the intersectionality of concerns of racial purity (tied to eugenics and population growth) in the regimes I mention that incite physical and psychic violence against those marked as sexually dissident. Homosexuality as signifier, its rupture of social categories, and its threat to national and social cohesion in the representation of nationhood and empire situates it as a discursive and social phenomenon. At the same time, in the academic sphere, queer work challenges not only social normativities, categories, and institutions, but—as a mode of analysis—exerts pressure on the strict demarcations of disciplinary borders that establish and separate intellectual turf, insiders and outsiders working within disciplines, and disciplinary "purity." These disciplinary borders are similarly challenged and begin to rupture at the innovative and productive conjunction of Holocaust and queer studies.

2

The Racialization of Sexuality: Rethinking Same-Sex Desire within Nazi Juridical Discourse

An alternative to the Jewish/non-Jewish debate prevalent in Holocaust scholarship has been to differentiate the various groups of Holocaust victims persecuted for *what they were* in terms of their genetic or cultural origins (e.g., Jews, Roma, Sinti, Slavs), those persecuted for *what they did* (e.g., homosexuals, resistance fighters, political prisoners), and those persecuted for *what they refused to do* (e.g., pacifists, Jehovah's witnesses).[1] While this may help to provide a more viable lens for understanding the different victims of nazi persecution, it proves problematic in the specific instance of homosexual victims. In assuming that gay men and lesbians were simply persecuted for "what they did," one uncritically reduces lesbian and gay subjectivity to erotic acts alone. That assumption unwittingly supports some, but not all, nazi and more contemporary homophobic views that same-sex eroticism is simply a behavior that is freely and consciously chosen and thereby susceptible to, and deserving of, legal consequences, ranging from the refusal to inscribe same-sex affectional bonds on the social register, to psychic and/or physical assault, to criminal liability. More important, such a distinction forecloses the possibility of accounting for the signifying practices that constituted gay and lesbian subjects as other under National Socialism as discussed in the previous chapter. As Malcolm Bowie reminds us in speaking of the post-Freudian subject, it is no longer feasible to construe subjectivity as "a substance endowed with qualities or a fixed shape possessing dimensions," as is often the way in which homosexuals have been represented in Holocaust research. Rather, Bowie continues, it is far more productive to understand (sexual) subjectivity as "a series of events within language, a procession of turns, tropes, and inflections" (76).

Certainly the array of memoirs and testimonies of gay and lesbian survivors has helped Holocaust research move away from homosexuality as a phenomenon to be encountered to a better appreciation of the actual, lived experiences of homophobic victimization under nazism. Yet these works, while intensely compelling, still confine sexual desire largely to the private sphere of the individual and represent the effects of—and responses to—homophobic persecution in very personal terms. It is important to build on this work and broaden understandings of nazi power by theorizing it in terms of its (re)organization of sexual life and its wider social and political implications, by asking, as Dagmar Herzog notes, citing Marcuse, "how central the politicization of the previously more private realm of sexuality was to the Nazis' political agenda, and how it was that sexual arousal could become a mechanism for social manipulation" ("Hubris and Hypocrisy" 4).[2]

Instead of reducing lesbian and gay subjectivities to felt or enacted desires or to individual identities and lived experiences alone, I wish to argue that lesbian and gay subjectivities need to be interpreted and understood in relation to juridical practices under National Socialism and their precedents in German cultural history. That is, they require examination through historically specific cultural and political discourses, symbols, and meanings, and through the ways in which the perceived threat against such heterosexually-encoded structures as the family, reproductive politics, erotic pleasure, and racial and national fantasy incited persecution and violence against lesbians and gay men. The nazis themselves seemed keenly aware of the potential ambiguities and contingencies in precisely defining homosexuality in their extension of Paragraph 175 of the Reich Penal Code legislated in 1935. The original penal code (1871) criminalized "unnatural sex acts" specifically between males or by humans with animals and punished these with imprisonment. Article 6 of the amendment to Paragraph 175, which was passed on June 28, 1935, broadened the range of the so-called *unnatural sex act* in the previous wording (often synonymous with anal intercourse, but Paragraph 175 also included oral penetration, intercrural sex, or self-gratification in the presence of another man) by replacing this term with that of *sex offense*. The addition of Paragraph 175A allowed for imprisonment of up to ten years, or not less than three months, for men who threatened to commit acts of violence toward other men in order to compel them to engage in a sex offense; men who abused relations of dependence based on service, employment, or subordination; men who seduced young men under the age of twenty-one to commit a sex offense with them; men who committed sex offenses with other men in public; and homosexual prostitutes.[3] In other words, the use of the term *sexual offense*, according to Günter Grau, not only designated an intercourse-like act (anal or oral penetration or intercrural sex involving ejaculation), but included any kind of sexual self-gratification in the presence of another man. This could include physical contact between men "with sexual intent" (including the snuggling together of two naked male bodies) (64) and made expression of feeling between men (Oosterhuis, "Male Bonding" 249) and homoerotic fantasy and thought (Feig 163) criminal offenses under the revised code.[4] Moreover, the revision in the law was applied retroactively, in terms of the prosecution of cases, for offenses committed prior to 1935.

The shift from Paragraph 175 to Paragraph 175A was a shift from sodomy to specific punishable acts that could include kissing, embracing, touching, and homosexual fantasies as articulated in private conversations and letters. While there were persecutions against lesbians, lesbian sex was not specifically written into the penal code in Germany, either in Paragraph 175 or in its revision, but there were sufficient debates among nazi jurists about whether or not to criminalize sex between women.[5] The change in law not only criminalized gay men for *enacted* desires, that is, for what they did, but for *articulated* desires as well, that is, for their expressions of their feelings, thoughts, and desires for other men. But while the broadening of the law helped set the groundwork for increased persecution in 1935 and exposed homosexuality in the public sphere by making it more detectable, the juridical surveillance and management of same-sex affectional and erotic bonds need to be connected to broader nazi social policies, specifically surrounding population policy tied to racial hygiene, the elimination of social degeneracy, and the policing of gender tied to the maintenance of rigid distinctions between the sexes and to the procreative responsibility of Aryan citizens. It is important, therefore, to understand homophobia as an effect of nazi power.

In spite of George Mosse's widely accepted claim in *Nationalism and Sexuality* that nazi fascism was profoundly occupied with questions of sexual propriety, it would be amiss to assume that the fear and hatred of homosexuality was simply rooted in sexual prudery. As Dagmar Herzog points out, since the central heuristic in the Third Reich was anti-Semitism as a central meaning-making system, it was the *racialization* of sexuality that enabled and instantiated heightened persecutions of homosexuals and portrayed them as enemies of the state ("Hubris and Hypocrisy" 9); that is, homosexuality was regarded as another form of degeneracy that needed to be eradicated in the name of the morality of the *Volk* and the superiority of the Nordic race. This specific connection is articulated in one of Heinrich Himmler's secret directives to the Secret State Police Bureau: "Homosexual men are enemies of the state and should be treated as such. What is at stake is the recovery of the German national body [and] the preservation and boosting of the strength of the German *Volk*" (qtd. in Grau, *Hidden Holocaust?* 96).[6]

At the same time, however, nazi homophobia, as a vector of domination, was deeply rooted in German society both predating and outliving the nazis. It can be linked to attempts at the preservation of bourgeois respectability and to idealized notions of masculinity and femininity, that is, to the enforcement of that matrix of heterosexuality whereby bodies, genders, and desires are "naturalized" to the point that "for bodies to cohere and make sense, there must be a stable sex expressed through a stable gender…that is oppositionally and hierarchically defined through the compulsory practice of heterosexuality" (Butler, *Gender Trouble* 194n). The extension of Paragraph 175 in 1935, the rhetoric surrounding such major events in the nazi persecution of homosexuals as the Röhm Purge of 1934,[7] the establishment of the Reichszentrale zur Bekämpfung der Homosexualität und der Abtreibung (Central Reich Office for Combating Homosexuality and Abortion) in 1936, and Himmler's Bad Tölz speech in 1937 point not only to the racialization of sexuality, but also to the reinforcement of strict regimes of gender in relation to the wider anti-Semitic project of nazism. It is not possible, therefore, to understand fully nazi homophobia apart from pre-existent, but heightened, ideologies of race, gender, and social respectability under National Socialism. Similarly, but in ways not reducible to Jews, homosexuals—as George Mosse has pointed out—were thought to use their sexuality as a weapon against society (*Nationalism and Sexuality* 151). Jews, like homosexuals, were also marked by sexual excess, seen as being unable to control their lusts and passions. For Jews, according to Mosse, this meant that their uncontrolled sexual drives were directed toward gentile women, corrupting Aryan mothers and thereby preventing the birth of healthy German children (*Nationalism and Sexuality* 140). In homosexuals, under the same logic, uncontrolled physical urges were directed toward other men, which weakened society because pleasure was put ahead of the duty to reproduce. Without assuming, then, that homosexual oppression was simply reducible to the oppression experienced by Jewish victims of nazi power, homosexuality was read nonetheless in racialized terms. Indeed, as Stefan Micheler sums up, the nazis relied on deep-seated homophobia that had preceded their rise to power, and they read homosexuality as a threat to revered notions of bourgeois respectability on the one hand, and as incompatible with the gender ideology of a patriarchal, heteronormative society on the other (98). Homosexuality under nazism must be understood, then, as bifurcated, that is, it must be read and interpreted along the twin axes of racial and gender power, both of which were infused by fixed norms of social respectability.

Most historians agree that the trauma of German defeat after World War I and the further weakening of Germany following economic depression—especially increased mass unemployment and rising vagrancy between 1929 and 1933—exacerbated further the production of discourses on eugenics and racial hygiene by the German state alongside complementary discourses on "degeneracy," already developing steadily in the early twentieth century within the psychiatric and medical professions and eventually used socially as diagnostic tools and applied to those who fell outside of accepted norms of respectability. Whether seen in judicial terms by state prosecutors, judges, or social welfare administrators as a form of criminal conduct requiring harsher penalties for repeat offenders, or as a medical or psychiatric pathology that could or could not be "cured," homosexuals were, in both contexts, relegated to the status of social outsiders. The nazi state viewed them as criminals who seduced and corrupted the young and as "population zeros" who contributed to a declining birth rate in Germany by not fulfilling their obligation to the reproduction of the race and the welfare of the nation. Medical practitioners, meanwhile, regarded them as unhealthy degenerates who could not control their physical urges. In medical literature going back to the end of the nineteenth century, images of Jews and homosexuals often run parallel. As George Mosse notes, both were portrayed as prone to hysteria (often with nervous bodily distortions) and feminized through descriptive characteristics (in the authoritative voice of medical science), such as tone of voice and bodily movements more appropriate to women than to men (*Fascist Revolution* 64).[8] The social use of medical discourses helped relegate homosexuals (and other groups) to the constitutive outside of national belonging as a threat to the economic and political well-being of the nation-state. This fusion of the medical and juridical spheres, through what Richard Evans has referred to as "the medicalization of penal policy," can be traced to the information-gathering and monitoring activities of the social welfare system before the advent of the Third Reich. But the nazis, Evans insists, fused much more extremely and more ostensively the various discourses of medicine and social administration as a means to assert further and intensify the boundaries between society and its outcasts (38). In this sense, race and sexuality are linked in regimes that tolerate no ambiguities between racial differences (most obvious under National Socialism in Germany or apartheid in South Africa) to the extent that the sexuality of so-called inferior races and social degenerates can be used as a means to infect the health of the nation.

While racism is a modern ideology that originated in the eighteenth century through such disciplines as anthropology, phrenology, and physiognomy, which gave the veneer of scientific certainty and became more elaborated in the nineteenth century, helping to shape the idea of rootedness and sense of belonging evident in nationalism and sharpening the distinctions between nations

(Mosse, *Fascist Revolution* 55), it is erroneous to explain nazi racism exclusively in terms of nineteenth-century medical discourses and scientific racism rooted in Enlightenment thinking that are often invoked as its ideological precedent. Andrew Hewitt has argued that nazi racism did not merely assert the superiority of one race over another, despite the evidence of nazi rhetoric to the contrary, but presented the Jew as an inferior historical condition. Late eighteenth-and nineteenth-century theories of scientific racism translated into policies of "management" of the racially different so as to maintain strategies of social exclusion, but, according to Hewitt, annihilation and genocide under nazism no longer depended on mere management (*Political Inversions* 124). This is an important distinction between Jews and other social outsiders such as homosexuals, so as not to conflate anti-Semitism and the Final Solution with the social management of homosexuals, some of whom were given the opportunity to reform,[9] while still accounting for overarching nazi preoccupations with racial hygiene, respectability, and immutability. Yet, at the same time, both Jews and homosexuals were marked with excessive sexuality: homosexuality was interpreted in racialized terms, and Jews were often feminized and accused of using their sexuality against the social order. Similarly, nineteenth-century stereotypes of homosexuals as weak and effeminate were redeployed in nazi propaganda directly aimed at homosexuals, the trace of which can also be found in nazi propaganda against Jews.

Himmler's establishment of the Reichszentrale zur Bekämpfung der Homosexualität und der Abtreibung within Gestapo Headquarters in Berlin on October 26, 1936, was not only part of a reorganization of the criminal police and a phase of heightened inscription and prosecution of homosexuals through what Geoffrey Giles refers to as "centralized police intervention" ("Homosexual Panic" 242) made possible by the legal groundwork set up through the extension of Paragraph 175,[10] but even more prominently linked homosexuality with racial and population politics. Preserving the sovereignty and purity of the Aryan race meant not only protecting it from inferior races and other enemies of the state, but also ensuring that the German birth rate flourished. Homosexual sex and a high number of abortions were blamed for stunting population growth, and, according to Himmler, posed a serious danger to population policy and public health.[11] The most important task of the Reichszentrale zur Bekämpfung der Homosexualität und der Abtreibung came under "Task Group B, Department 3: Immorality" alongside other similar registration departments within Group B also concerned with immorality and forming part of the executive side of the Reich Criminal Police Bureau. These included the Combating of Obscene Pictures, Writings, and Advertisements; the Combating of Drug Offenses; Combating of the International White Slave Trade; and so on. The main task of the Reich Office for the Combating of Homosexuality and Abortion was, according to Günter Grau, to quantify, index, and compare relevant data through an elaborate, centralized index card system to keep track of those suspected and convicted of homosexuality, while also attempting to obtain personal details on their sexual partners (*Hidden Holocaust?* 104). The Reich Office also registered transvestites, wage abortionists (including medical doctors, midwives, and healers), and controlled the manufacture and sale of birth control items. Police were trained in how to identify gay men, largely based on stereotypes of gender inversion, and where to catch them engaging in sexual cruising, expressing verbal or physical affection for one another, fondling, or engaging in sexual acts (such as in public parks, baths, and toilets and in railway stations, bars, and hotels), all punishable under the revised Reich Penal Code. While Himmler and officials at the Reichszentrale insisted that homosexual offenses came under local police jurisdiction, the special department of the Secret State Police, which began the task of registering and prosecuting homosexuals in 1934 until its authority was expanded and centralized under the newly created Reichszentrale zur Bekämpfung der Homosexualität und der Abtreibung two years later (see note 10) and remained in existence until the beginning of World War II, close links were established and maintained with the Gestapo. According to Grau, the Gestapo had to be called in if the offender's homosexuality represented a serious threat to population policy or public health (*Hidden Holocaust?* 105), such as in cases of congenital homosexuality, rent boys and male prostitutes, homosexual offenses involving juveniles, and homosexual offenses committed within the Catholic clergy, especially if these threatened or endangered children or youth.

The Reichszentrale zur Bekämpfung der Homosexualität und der Abtreibung was a bureaucratic body that played a key role in the nazi pogrom against homosexuality, yet there is disagreement on how precisely and consistently it functioned. Stefan Micheler, for instance, argues that the Reich Office only required certain groups to register with it: members of the Party and affiliated organizations, Wehrmacht soldiers, Jews, clergy and members of religious orders, and those who occupied important social positions prior to the nazi rise to power in 1933, supposedly so that any suspicious charges of homosexuality could be checked and recorded, though Micheler does not say so directly. Micheler acknowledges that local police officials often passed on the names of individual homosexuals to the Reichszentrale, but argues that no attempt was made to establish a list or official registry of homosexuals (109). While I do accept Geoffrey Giles's argument that the "implementation of policies against homosexuals was neither consistent nor unfailingly rigorous" ("Denial of

Homosexuality" 289) as it was against Jews, the function of the Reichszentrale and its connection to population politics and racial hygiene cannot be underestimated. While there were uncertainties among nazi leaders centered around the etiology of homosexuality, and a differentiation between so-called congenital and "opportunistic" homosexuality, what is certain is that surveillance and arrests rose sharply in the years following the setting up of the new Reich Office. In the period between 1937 and 1939, 90,000 men and youth were registered as suspected homosexuals or as presumed partners (Röll 9), and an unpublished report of the Central Reich Office for Combating Homosexuality and Abortion indicates the number of men sentenced for crimes against Paragraph 175 or 175A (or for corrupting youth under Paragraphs 174 or 176) to be nearly 43,000 between 1936 and 1939, that is, from the year the Reich Office was formed until the start of the war in September 1939.[12] Despite the inconsistency in views on the precise function of the Reich Office, Grau's point that there is no proof that it specifically directed and planned the persecution of homosexuals, as it only had a staff of eighteen employees ("Final Solution" 342), is an important one. Certainly denunciations by neighbors, family members, or co-workers facilitated the work of the Reich Office. Micheler observes that between 1936 and 1937, more than 25 percent of lower court cases involving Paragraph 175 and 175A violations in Hamburg were the result of third-party denunciations, as were 30 percent of all court cases from 1933 to 1945 (126).[13] But this should not blind one to the role of the Reichszentrale zur Bekämpfung der Homosexualität und der Abtreibung in the overall campaign against homosexuals in particular and in overall nazi population policy in general. Nor should it obscure the ways in which acts of bureaucratic registration preceded and further enabled acts of criminal prosecution in the name of preserving the purity and respectability of the Aryan race and the strength of the German state.

Closely related to epistemes of racial hygiene under nazism was a preoccupation with social respectability and gender and sexual normalcy, both of which can be traced to the cultural logic of late nineteenth-century modernity. The marking of more intense social divisions and the shift in cultural values at the time, which Giles attributes, in part, to the rise of socialism and a greater role for women in public life ("Denial of Homosexuality" 288), and to medical work on homosexuality that shifted its study, as Foucault notes, from that of a temporary aberration to an identity category (Foucault 43), were reflected in considerable gender and sexual anxiety among middle-class Germans in the late nineteenth-century ("Denial of Homosexuality" 288). These social and epistemological shifts helped to demarcate more overt boundaries between what was considered to be normal and abnormal, positioning the figure of the homosexual, as Mosse notes, as the antithesis of respectability (*Nationalism and Sexuality* 37). Because sodomy, masturbation beyond adolescence, and other forms of non-procreative sexual practice have a history linked to deviancy, impotence, and depopulation, it was also assumed that the link to deviancy could create a kind of secrecy that could threaten the health of the nation-state. This might occur through a lack of civic responsibility by practitioners of such vices at one extreme, or through a conscious, intentional conspiracy against the state at the other (Mosse, *Nationalism and Sexuality* 29).[14] So there was an historical precedent for the pathologization of homosexuality and the social proliferation of homophobia prior to the rise of nazi power. As Giles reminds us, a nearly hysterical opposition to homosexuality was not only peculiar to the nazi era but is found in other conservative regimes where sexual differences can disturb the image of society as (sexually) homogeneous ("Denial" 288).

The link of medical and juridical discourses to scrutinize and regulate homosexuality socially, which also helped to instantiate the paradigmatic shift in thinking from specific acts of sodomy to homosexual identity in the mid-nineteenth century and contributed to a history of sexual anxiety around homosexuality and other sexual deviances later in the nineteenth and early twentieth centuries, implies a slight rethinking of Foucault. Hewitt quite rightly notes that there was never really a complete break between homosexuality, understood in terms of an identity, and its dependence on the sodomitical act insofar as the identity that is socially and historically constructed is one that remains fixated on the specificity of the act itself. In other words, according to Hewitt, how can homosexual identity, as discursively constructed within medicine and the law, assert itself over and beyond its instantiation in any specific form of homosexual sex (*Political Inversions* 150–51)? Hewitt's point is an important one and does not undermine or contradict my earlier contention that reading homosexuals as persecuted by the nazis simply for what they did (that is, for specific sexual acts) has its limits. Even though the extension of Paragraph 175 in the Reich Penal Code criminalized a range of behaviors and expressions of feelings and thoughts not necessarily reducible to anal penetration as the primary signifier of homosexuality, the sodomitical trace nonetheless remained and circulated under National Socialism. It bore the mark of social degeneracy in defense of middle-class norms of morality pertaining to the body and sexual behavior, marriage, and family life under heteronormativity, and solidified social distinctions between normality and abnormality. Normal/abnormal distinctions were especially intensified by right-wing opposition to the new public visibility of homosexuality under the Weimar Republic. Under National Socialism, immediate measures were taken to maintain the normal/abnormal split through the banning of pornography (February 1933), the destruction of Magnus Hirschfeld's Sexual Science Institute (May 1933), and raids on and closing of gay bars in Berlin (1933, 1934) following the nazi accession to power in January 1933. Just as nazi homophobia cannot be separated from nazi theories of racial purity and racial hygiene, notions of sexual degeneracy were not unrelated to nazi racist thinking. As Mosse notes, stereotyped depictions of sexual degenerates were transferred nearly intact to "inferior races," who inspired the same fears of unbridled sexuality to the extent that blacks—and especially Jews—were marked by excessive, uncontrollable sexuality (*Nationalism and Sexuality* 36).

Concern for middle-class respectability and sexual propriety did limit erotic autonomy under National Socialism, as Mosse and others have indicated, but it would be reductive, as I suggested earlier, to interpret nazi views of sexuality as exclusively repressive. While same-sex sexualities were certainly racialized and homophobia became rampant under nazi rule, and while sexual excess and deviancy were projected onto what the nazis considered to be inferior races, the repressive public discourse on sexuality was also sexually provocative. For instance, nazi sexual politics did provide, as Herzog argues, inducements to pre- and extra-marital sexuality and other forms of (hetero)sexual pleasure to those broad sectors of society that were not persecuted, reflecting, therefore, not simply a backlash against the progressivism of Weimar, but a redefinition and expansion of those pre-existing liberalizing trends ("Hubris and Hypocrisy" 6, 9). There is also evidence of sexual liberalism in nazi campaigns against the authority of the church in the Catholic regions of Germany. The Cloister Trials of April and May 1937 centered on the arrests and staged trials (deliberately open to the media and press) of Catholic clergymen, priests, monks, Christian brothers, and lay persons accused of unnatural sex acts and of seducing children and abusing lines of trust, all of which were punishable under the penal code. Yet the purpose of these trials was not merely to expose homosexuality within the Catholic hierarchy, but to undermine its authority to the extent that the church often represented a competing belief system by comparison with nazi ideology. One such difference was church teachings on sexuality and morality, in that it took a repressive stance toward masturbation, extra-marital sex, illegitimacy, and non-procreative sexual pleasure within marriage, all of which the nazis read as imposing sinful drives onto natural processes,[15] and as an attempt to undermine the "vibrant" and "life-affirming" German and Nordic people (Herzog, "Hubris and Hypocrisy" 10–11).

Sexual morality, prudery, and repression were articulated through anti-Semitism, homophobia, racism, and intolerance of the physically disabled or mentally ill. But within the confines of Aryan heterosexuality (which would have had to be free of physical or mental handicap), a different kind of sexual and reproductive politics that encouraged sexual openness and experimentation emerged that was tied to the goal of strengthening the nation-state through population growth. While sexual pleasures did not necessarily need to be procreative and were not limited to the confines of marriage within Aryan heterosexuality, many nazi doctors also defended child and adolescent masturbation and criticized the social repression of women's sexual agency in an effort to condone officially sexual pleasure and produce supposedly happier marriages, wider outlets for (hetero)sexual activity, and possibly a higher birth rate. Rather than reading heterosexual marriage (as stable, monogamous, and tied exclusively to procreation) as the mirror image of homophobic readings of homosexuality, nazi defenses of sexual emancipation and pleasure for Aryans remained somewhat at odds with its attacks on homosexuality as a pursuit of pleasure without control of the physical passions and without regard for the welfare of the state. The public defense of heterosexual family life, which was to be protected from homosexuality and other enemies of the state, and appeals to middle-class norms of social respectability based on the image (or perhaps more accurately, the fantasy) of the stability of marriage, ironically may have resulted in a weakening and undermining of marriage and family life under National Socialism through the (hetero)sexual pleasures that were encouraged.

A site of further ambiguity and contradiction concerning sexuality in relation to nazi ideologies and standards of practice concerning same-sex-desiring men relates to the legacy of the homoerotic *Männerbund* and the role of male homosociality within National Socialism, particularly within the elite corps of the nazi SS. Harry Oosterhuis has documented the historical significance of romantic friendships between men within the German cultural tradition—*Freundesliebe*—dating back to the mid-eighteenth century, which often included a passionate and sensual component that enhanced the intellectual and emotional ties between men. But Oosterhuis points out that these close bonds were later superseded by the confinement of emotional and physical intimacy to marriage and to family life in the second half of the nineteenth century (Oosterhuis, "Homosexual Emancipation" 8–11), and by the medicalization of same-sex love at around the same time, which I have already mentioned.

The *Gemeinschaft der Eigenen* (for friendship and freedom), an ideological group begun by Adolf Brand and a few of his friends in 1903,[16] was a later variation of romantic male friendship tradition (*Freundesliebe*) that had flourished in Germany between 1750 and 1850. It was formed as an oppositional response to new meanings attached to male homosocial bonds and emotional attachments by the influence of medical discourses, including Magnus Hirschfeld's distinction between the friendships of heterosexual men and erotic, or homosexual, same-sex attachments.[17] In the very beginning of the twentieth century, the *Gemeinschaft der Eigenen* glorified the love of male friends as a way to rise above bourgeois mediocrity and materialism. It also saw the struggles for equality among workers and women at the time as a feminization of society, again in opposition to Hirschfeld, who regarded equal rights for women as in the interests of homosexuals (Oosterhuis, introduction to "Political Issues and the Rise of Nazism" 185–86), most likely because groups for both homosexual and women's emancipation were by and large committed to broadened conceptualizations of gender and freedom from the tyranny of fixed gender roles that could undermine erotic autonomy. Yet, healthy culture, according to the *Gemeinschaft der Eigenen*, based on male bonding, was inherently masculinist, and also implied aristocratic (elitist) racist and misogynist leanings, showing that historically homosexual movements have not always been aligned with leftist, progressive social movements. The *Gemeinschaft der Eigenen*, in fact, believed—according to Oosterhuis—that German genius could be saved from decadence and decline by a homoerotic male culture (introduction to "Political Issues and the Rise of Nazism" 187–88). The social conservatism of the group, and the importance it placed on male bonding, conventional masculinity, and the maintenance of gender differences, aligned it more with the social goals of German nationalism, and eventually National Socialism, albeit for its celebratory views of male homosexuality.

Yet the legacy of the *Männerbund*, in the form of the idealization of male friendships (which is distinct to German cultural history), was carried over into National Socialism, particularly within the ranks of the nazi leadership and not without its homoerotic appeal (through its celebration of masculinity, male physical beauty, and masculine militaristic vigor in images of the *Sturmabteilung* or nazi storm troopers) to those within the nazi ranks and to gay—and quite possibly some heterosexual—men within German society.[18] The homoeroticism that was evoked by the worship of masculinity brought about a tension between German nationalism and respectability, which the nazis tried to keep under control through the Röhm Purge in 1934 and heightened prosecutions for homosexuality within the SS and police—including punishment by death by Hitler's decree in 1941. What appealed to National Socialism, however, were German ideals of male physical and mental strength, heroism and self-sacrifice, and male solidarity and superiority over those deemed as other, all of which were important for the training of the body and the will. Instead of publicly acknowledging the fraught, intertwined, and inextricable links between male homosocial bonds and homoeroticism, the nazis preferred, as

Giles notes, the term *Kameradschaft* (comradeship) to describe the life-or-death dependability between men, especially as it occurred in the trenches between soldiers during World War I ("Homosexual Panic" 238). The shift to the term *Kameradschaft* also attempted to disavow any homoerotic connotation, since this would mark a departure from masculinity and a betrayal of the bonds and trust between men, and would weaken, rather than strengthen, such bonds if they were to become eroticized.[19] The *Männerbund* ideal, certainly echoed in the *Gemeinschaft der Eigenen*, did not rule out marriage, as long as it allowed for the maintenance of the differentiation of gender roles, a point I shall take up shortly, whereby the role of women was restricted to the domestic sphere so that men could devote themselves to the more serious pursuits of activities concerning culture and politics with other men (Oosterhuis, "Male Bonding" 243–44). Such gender differentiation, containing the trace of male bonding and friendships in German cultural history prior to the Third Reich, both supported the family (to the extent that the family served population policy under nazism), yet disrupted it, to the extent that, as Oosterhuis notes, "close emotional ties with the family were not conducive to the role which the man in close alliance with other men was obliged to fulfill in Nazism" ("Male Bonding" 253–54). While homosexuals were persecuted as a threat to family life, the nazi social differentiation of gender and the ties of comradeship expected between men ironically served to undermine the family as a private sphere, as well as curtail the development of close emotional ties between spouses and between parents and their children.

Finally, as has been implied in my discussion thus far, strict demarcations between the genders were put in place under nazi power, especially since hegemonic masculinity and manliness (and therefore physical strength and virility, with which they were associated) were grafted onto German national identity. As Mosse notes in *Nationalism and Sexuality*, the idea of masculinity, including standards of male beauty thought to be inherited from classical Greece, was equated with health, vigor, order, reason, and control of the passions and put into the service of European nationalisms (31) as they developed in the late eighteenth century. Thus masculinity and femininity were reflected in family and social life and "reaffirmed as imperatives of the modern age" (24). Under such a paradigm, women had a symbolic role of immutability rather than progress, and, as Mosse argues, provided a backdrop against which men determined the fate of nations (*Nationalism and Sexuality* 23). This fits with what I mentioned earlier in the context of the legacy of the *Männerbund* ideal (in the *Gemeinschaft der Eigenen* in particular), which confined women to the domestic sphere and valued the homosocial relations between men (to the extent that men could devote themselves to all aspects of political and cultural life), reinforced a division of labor based on gender, and ensured social respectability. Not only were women largely confined to domestic servitude under such nationalist paradigms, but nineteenth-century medical discourses also characterized women as prone to fits of hysteria because of a weakened physical and nervous state. The growing obsession with racial hygiene that developed in France, Italy, Germany, and the United States in the late nineteenth century enabled the social projection of feminine characteristics onto homosexuals and Jews, making them responsible for the breakdown of the sex/gender codes of heteronormativity on which the social order and social respectability were based. Thus, not only was the social inscription of Jews and homosexuals racialized and medicalized, as I have already argued, but also gendered to the extent that these groups were specifically denied masculine agency. Masculinity, indeed a hypermasculinity, was inseparable from the identity of the Third Reich, especially within the nazi leadership, and feminizing homosexuals and Jews made them stand out in sharp contrast to the militaristic character of the nazi movement and state. While Giles seems to assume that the militaristic image of nazism reflected a need for manliness and the sign of masculine authority ("Homosexual Panic" 238), I would suggest, from a slightly more queer perspective, that such hypermasculine imagery was used as a cover, or possibly as a suture, for the homoerotic potential of such homosocial relations. In essence, it was promoted as a way of creating and sustaining the *public* illusion of physical strength and virility, disavowing any visible signs of homosexuality (given the historical connection of the *Gemeinschaft der Eigenen* to the *Männerbund* tradition in Germany), and as a way of maintaining socially constructed divisions of gender enforced at the time.[20]

Nazism brutally enforced the matrix of intelligibility through which bodies cohere and make sense, so that—using Judith Butler's theory of gender performativity—sexuality was kept under surveillance "through the *policing* and the *shaming* of gender" (*Bodies That Matter* 238; emphasis added), through heightened and violent social strategies of regulation, social abjection, and normalization linked to racial and population politics and to rhetorical appeals to aspirations toward social respectability. What the attention to failed or abject gender meant for homosexuals was not simply the clinical identification of a pathological disorder or disease, but, within the social domain, it represented a visible mark of un-Germanness, a loss of Aryan status in the case of white Nordic homosexuals (and a further proof of degeneracy and racial inferiority for those groups already marked as social outsiders, especially Jewish homosexuals, who were doubly stigmatized). Finally, gender dysfunction also signified in the nationalist imaginary as an identification with degeneracy, that is, a failure to identify with normative masculinity and manliness and therefore with the nation and a social order already conceived as masculine and under threat by a rapidly changing world.

The nazi pogrom against homosexuals must be seen not only in terms of the specific laws against homosexuality and specific and individual acts of persecution, but within the larger frame of the nazi/Aryan principle of the eradication of differences, that is, what Wolfgang Röll has referred to as a "race destroying manifestation of degeneracy" insofar as the eradication of homosexuality from the public sphere would enable sexuality to work in the service of population growth and eugenics so that Germany could take its deserved position of world power and global hegemony (7–8). Homophobia under National Socialism, then, cannot be understood as a mere form of domination against homosexuals, but as operating socially at the nexus of a range of signifying practices related to racial politics, eugenics, homosociality (as a historical/cultural precedent and as a characteristic of nazi fascist power), social respectability, and gender fixity. Yet a crucial difference from Jewish persecution was that punishments for homosexuality were not always consistently applied. They often varied in severity as a result of disagreements among nazi officials and medical doctors regarding the etiology of homosexuality, that is, the degree to which homosexuality was regarded as a behavioral or psychic disorder, or as a genetic trait that could be infectious to the health of the nation. While the nazis dismissed Freud and Hirschfeld as Jews and were similarly dismissive of sexology, there was great disagreement among nazi officials and eugenicists on the issue of the genetic or social origins of homosexuality, which was never resolved under National Socialism and led to inconsistencies in the persecutions of homosexuals.[21] In addition, there were further inconsistencies surrounding the application of the full extent of the law against homosexuals who had already fought for their country during the war or who had family connections to the nazi elite, including to Himmler himself (Giles, "Denial" 289–90). As a practical matter during the war, it also became difficult to investigate and prosecute homosexuals and maintain the ideological apparatus of homophobia, though other evidence suggests that the police were still pursuing individuals suspected of homosexuality as late as February 1945 with Germany on the brink of collapse (Giles, "Denial" 279). Another inconsistency was that Himmler decreed on October 29, 1937, a special regulation that artists and actors not be detained for allegations pertaining to unnatural sex acts without his prior approval, unless they were actually caught in the act (Grau, *Hidden Holocaust?* 137–38). These contradictions were also evident in the practices of concentration camps in which homosexuals were interred. Jonathan Friedman notes that two homosexual realities prevailed in camps; there were situational same-sex couplings among otherwise heterosexual prisoners (including ones between prisoners and capos, who were prisoners responsible for work detachments) that were largely ignored, and there was the overall brutal treatment of homosexual prisoners (24).[22] Further, while there is a significant difference between National Socialist anti-homosexual rhetoric and ideology on the one hand, and the day-to-day practice of actual persecutions of homosexuals on the other (given some of the inconsistencies in prosecutions and punishments just mentioned), some scholars have justifiably argued that what the nazis had in mind was not the eradication of all homosexuals, but the eradication of the sign of homosexuality, that is, homosexuality as signifier, from the public sphere (Grau, "Final Solution" 340; Micheler 96). These inconsistencies and differences, however, while obviously not applying under the rubric or practice of nazi anti-Semitism or to the goals of the Final Solution, should not lessen the historical realities of homophobic terror and violence under nazism, nor blind us to the ways in which nazi homophobia is intertwined with the politics of racial domination, population policy, and gender simultaneously produced under nazi rule.

3

The Politics of Gender Difference: Lesbian Existence under the Third Reich

The racialization of (homo)sexuality under nazism left little room for erotic autonomy to the extent that the nazis were keenly obsessed with the production of genetically fit Aryans. It would be amiss, however, to presume that all forms of non-marital or non-procreative (hetero)sexuality were characterized as illicit; such was not the case if these sexual relations occurred among and between those deemed to be racially pure Aryans. But homosexuality, along with bestiality (Paragraph 175B under the revised penal code) and other forms of sexual "decadence," given nazi population and racial politics, was largely represented and codified as a Semitic invention under tropes of sexual waywardness and excess. Nazi propaganda linked homosexuality to the weakening of the German state; its juridical code targeted same-sex relations between men as susceptible to criminal prosecution, and many thousands of gay men under National Socialism were incarcerated in prisons and in concentration camps, assigned labor, used for medical experimentation, and even exterminated. Lesbians, on the other hand, while not always persecuted for their *sexuality* alone, as was the case for many gay men, could be susceptible to persecution through the axis of *gender*, that is, through non-conformity to the norms of gender, including marriage and the institution of heterosexuality, as well as for their political beliefs, insofar as they challenged the gender/sexual politics of the nazi state or nazi ideology in general.

Conventional wisdom in Holocaust research has stipulated quite consistently that lesbians were not as systematically persecuted by the nazis as were gay men. This was mainly because lesbian sex was not criminalized under Paragraph 175 of the Reich Penal Code, and because, as Claudia Schoppmann argues, the emotional bonds between women made it too difficult to distinguish between allowable and forbidden behaviors. In addition, the role of women in public life under the Third Reich was modest by comparison to (Aryan) gay men, who, as long as they remained closeted, would have had access to privilege and power, and therefore could have possibly threatened the rigid sex/gender norms of the nazi state in ways, perhaps, that women could not (Schoppmann, "The Campaign Against Homosexuality and Its Effects on Lesbians" 3–4). But the problem with so facilely dismissing the persecution of lesbians as insignificant because lesbian sex was not specifically criminalized is that one can be easily led to assume that lesbians were more or less invisible under National Socialism and suffered little feared or actual persecution as lesbians or more broadly as resistant women. Such a view risks further misrepresentation of the victims of nazism, given not only a paucity of available research on lesbians, but a broader precedent in Holocaust research that has not paid sufficient attention to the unique experiences of women, given a masculinist bias in narratives about Holocaust victims and survivors. In other words, since more research is still needed on the position(s) of lesbians, and in consideration of Judith Butler's important stipulation that sexuality is regulated in culture "through the policing and the shaming of gender" (*Bodies That Matter* 238), care must be taken to ensure that the axis of sexuality not override, and thereby obscure, the axis of gender in order to allow the specificity of lesbian difference (as distinct from gay men and heterosexual women) to emerge.

Until recently, the specific ways in which women might have experienced the Holocaust have been marginal in Holocaust research and underrepresented in the corpus of published testimonies and memoirs. Feminist research over the past two decades has sought to correct this historical elision by examining carefully the unique ways women may have experienced the Holocaust, especially since—as Esther Fuchs notes—nazi genocide was a systematic attack on the reproductive abilities of Jewish women (xi). Jewish women, and women of other so-called inferior races who were prevented from giving birth through forced abortion or sterilization; Aryan women, who were pressured to give up careers and to have children; the prevention of sexual liaisons and marriage between Aryans and races deemed inferior; women's experiences of molestation and rape; and the uses and abuses of prostitutes under nazism, especially in concentration camps, all affected women in unique ways and help broaden our understanding of nazi domination and fascist power. The fact that more Jewish women were deported and killed than Jewish men, that their chances of survival were less than for Jewish men, and that they were considered less valuable than Jewish men and more dangerous as mothers (and therefore more expendable), as Jonathan Friedman points out quoting Joan Miriam Ringelheim (42),[1] is also highly significant in terms of how we think about the Final Solution. This speaks to the need for more feminist work in Holocaust research as a way of differentiating further the various victims of nazi power and as a challenge to overall false assumptions that those persecuted by the nazis were constituted by a fundamental sameness.

The complementary problem to this historical elision of women's experience is the perpetuation of a masculinist bias in the narration of Holocaust history. Gender-specific experiences have been overlooked because women's lives, until as late as the 1990s, according to Joan Miriam Ringelheim, have been neutralized into a so-called human perspective, which erases the specificity of women's experiences ("The Unethical and the Unspeakable" 73). Ringelheim also identifies other areas of possible inquiry, including the specific abuses of women in gender-defined conditions, such as in the ghettos, camps, and resistant movements, and women's relationships with other women (81), the latter of which is one of the key questions of this chapter. The masculinist bias in interpreting the Holocaust, while exposing and critiquing nazi atrocities, has limited the range of women's experiences. Further, it often reproduces traditional sexist ideologies that cast women primarily in the domestic sphere and as disconnected from public life whether Aryan or not, and, in the specific case of Aryan women, as pure and beautiful and without subjective agency. It is as if, as Esther Fuchs acknowledges, the Holocaust were a mere disruption of the master narrative of family romance where women functioned only in the traditional sense (xii). But, of course, there are serious limits to such a view since the master narrative does not account for women's gains in education and employment prior to the rise of nazism, the enforced withdrawal of women from politics and other aspects of public life after the nazis came to power, the unique dangers posed to lesbians who were not defined by their relation to men, and the profound effects gender politics under nazism had on women's lives. The primacy of the (straight) male gaze—as narrator, as historian, as researcher—needs to be challenged further so that new and hitherto unasked questions can be asked of this particular history.

Gender, then, is an important axis of inquiry in interpreting the Holocaust, not because it distorts the Holocaust, a common criticism leveled against gender (and sexual) inquiry, as I noted in my introduction with regard to the symposium I attended on gender and the Holocaust, but because gender analysis puts pressure on a view of history as the mere recovery of a self-evident past, and because such an inquiry understands gender as a regime of power and as another lens with which to analyze nazi power. As Fuchs notes, the nazis produced an ideology of racist *and* sexist supremacy, and to ignore gender, as discussed in the previous chapter with respect to the nazis' maintenance of gender norms for men, is to remain oblivious to the profundity of nazi anti-Semitism and anti-humanism (ix). While gender analysis can bring the experiences of women under nazism away from the peripheries of Holocaust research and address the misogyny of the nazi regime as much feminist work has already done, gender can also be analyzed as a strategy of power, whereby certain groups were feminized, appropriated as weak and as a threat to the strength and masculinity of the German state. More important for my inquiry, gender analysis can expose how the fixing of gender norms for both women and men reinscribed heteronormative social relations, which were regarded as crucial to secure and preserve the stability of the regime. Gender analysis, in other words, can help provide different cultural interpretations of the Holocaust and question the (straight) male authorizing gaze/voice in its association with sovereignty and power, or as master narrator as Sara Horowitz points out (116–17). More important to my argument, further attention to gender can help to open up spaces of lesbian existence within Holocaust scholarship, instead of focusing exclusively on the axis of sexuality alone, which has been the predominant line of research in investigating the persecution of gay men.[2]

The period following World War I in Germany and the establishment of the more progressive Weimar Republic (1919–33) enabled a more vibrant visibility of gay male and lesbian subculture in the 1920s in such cities as Berlin, Hamburg, Cologne, Munich, and Frankfurt. For lesbians in particular, the establishment of organizations and bars and clubs and the circulation of the magazine *Die Freundin* (*Girlfriend*) between 1924 and 1933 were largely the effect of women's struggles earlier in the century for emancipation. Also influential were the efforts of Magnus Hirschfeld's Scientific Humanitarian Committee to raise public awareness of same-sex love and affectional bonds (for both sexes) and to gain public support for the repeal of Paragraph 175. Exploiting these two cultural strands—that of the rising social and cultural visibility of lesbians and Hirschfeld's analysis of sexual difference—Ruth Margarete Roellig in 1928 published the book *Berlins lesbische Frauen* (*Berlin's Lesbian Women*), which contained a preface or foreword (Vorwort) by Magnus Hirschfeld. In the preface, Hirschfeld says that one of the purposes of Roellig's book was to educate the public about women who were different and to help eradicate social prejudices about them (Roellig 10).[3] More important, Hirschfeld notes (as Roellig does herself by citing him later in the main text) that lesbians are not psychologically ill and neither socially inferior nor criminal, but often of great intelligence and artistic ability (Roellig 12, 23).[4] According to Roellig, as she further theorizes Hirschfeld's analysis of sexual difference, the male/female binary as the basis for intergender relations is not sufficient for all forms of affectional bonds. Exceptions to heterosexual bonds do not signify decadence or disease, but, as Roellig states in the French edition of her book "la caractérisation générale homme-femme n'est tout simplement plus suffisant.... Chez tous les organismes, les stades sexuels intermédiaires sont une manifestation parfaitement normale, loin d'être pathologique; leur apparition ne signale d'aucune manière une décadence corporelle" (23–25).[5] All of this, in addition to the unapologetic assertion (against dominant psychiatric and psychoanalytic thought of the time) that the passions of women who desire women are more exalted and spontaneous, less restrained than in normal heterosexual relations ["Ses passions, ses désirs, tout en elle est plus ardent, plus exalté, plus spontané, moins tempéré que dans une relation amoureuse normale"] (35), helped thrust the historical and social fact of lesbian existence into the public sphere against prejudices and anti-feminist, anti-homosexual stereotypes that were also part of the Weimar, especially as unemployment and inflation began to rise. Under the threat of a weakened economy, discussions of social and moral decadence became more pronounced. Ehrhard F.W. Eberhard, for instance—as Claudia Schoppmann notes—attacked the women's movement in his 1924 book *Die Frauenbewegung und ihre erotischen Grundlagen* (*The Women's Movement and Its Erotic Foundation*) and held the women's emancipation movement responsible for the real and imagined social ills of the Weimar (*Days of Masquerade* 6). Conservative social critics such as Eberhard argued that the women's emancipation movement was dangerous because it not only undermined prevailing social structures, but lesbians within it would "seduce" other women into withdrawing from men and from marriage.[6] As with male homosexuality, the juridical and medical spheres were linked and attempted to relegate lesbians to the constitutive outside of national belonging as early as the Weimar, though not with the same fervor and elevated tropes of racial hygiene that reduced gay men to racial enemies of the German state under nazism.

At the same time, women who wrote on the lesbian subculture under the Weimar, while simultaneously being positioned within it, not only sought to address and correct social prejudices, but situated "lesbian" as a social position, what Catharine R. Stimpson has described as "that invaluable way of being in, with, and against the world" (377) all at the same time. This is especially evident in the life stories—some autobiographical, others biographical—collected by Claudia Schoppmann in her examination of female homosexuality under nazism for her Ph.D. thesis. Schoppman's collected narratives are based on research in archives, unpublished texts, and interviews conducted in the late 1980s with women who survived the nazi years; her research was published in 1993 as *Zeit der Maskierung: Lebensgeschichten lesbischer Frauen im "Dritten Reich"* and translated into English and published in 1996 as *Days of Masquerade: Life Stories of Lesbians During the Third Reich*. The collected narratives attempt to establish and represent a sense of lesbian existence under the Weimar and under nazi rule as not reducible to erotic desire alone, though that was certainly part of it. For instance, Gertrude Sandmann, a painter of Jewish descent in Berlin, who was taken in by an "Aryan" family, noted in 1977 in a previous interview about her artistic work that a woman artist "should have a union that neither impedes her work nor hampers her development, that is, one containing much that is reciprocal and companionate.... Homosexuality is not merely a sexual variant, but a different attitude in many areas as a result of this predisposition" (Rentmeister; qtd. in Schoppmann, *Days of Masquerade* 79).[7] Similarly, in describing the life story of Elisabeth Zimmermann, another woman she researched, Schoppmann mentions the conflicts experienced by women who were forced to live a secret life but also desired self-determination and erotic autonomy (*Days of Masquerade* 117), showing that the repression of same-sex desire under the Third Reich did not simply obliterate it. Zimmermann, who also loved women, was assigned to the German embassy in Paris as a translator in its cultural affairs department during the war. While stationed in Paris for her assignment, she had a relationship with Anita from Berlin, who also worked at the German embassy developing and enlarging photographs for its press department between 1941 and 1944. Zimmermann recalls the first time she was kissed by Anita while caring for her during an illness:

> Somehow it just happened. It was as if she wanted to say, "Come here, I'll take you under my wing." ...I don't know if there were clubs or bars for homosexuals [in Paris]; we never went there. We often went to Parnasse or Montmartre or to the Boulevard St. Michel, but we didn't try to make friends or meet people. We were the *enemy*, so to speak. (Schoppmann, *Days of Masquerade* 120; emphasis added)

Zimmermann eventually married a man in 1944, though it was never a "real marriage." Yet, as Schoppmann notes from her 1987 conversation with her, Zimmermann could not really say why she had married: "So many things happen subconsciously and you can never actually put them into words. In any case, I never really tried. I just always followed my feelings and that was that.... And on top of that, the long period of secrecy, the repression, not letting anyone notice your true nature, or else I would have ended up in a concentration camp" (Schoppmann, *Days of Masquerade* 120–22).

What is revealed in the work of Roellig and the testimonials collected by Schoppmann (through previously published documents or direct interviews) from women who lived in Germany or France at the time is that a lesbian social space existed under the previous Weimar Republic and that it often functioned as a deliberate resistance to the pathologizing impulses coming from medical and psychiatric discourses, to tropes pertaining to social decadence coming from conservative social critics, and to bourgeois gender norms that undermined women's independence and erotic autonomy. This work also demonstrates the historical existence of a thriving lesbian subculture under the Weimar, never before present in Germany, with its own literature (Roellig's poems published in the magazine *Frauenliebe* and other work published in *Garçonne*) and its own clubs and meeting places (such as the Damenklub Violetta, and one of the oldest gay bars in Berlin, the Dorian Gray, which reserved certain days of the week for lesbians as discussed in Roellig's *Berlins lesbische Frauen*). But at the same time, it must be stressed that women also inhabited spaces of lesbian existence under the more repressive regime of the Third Reich, and it would be erroneous to assume that nazi power simply erased that existence or rendered it completely illegible, precisely since lesbian sex was not written into the penal code. When desire, whether felt or enacted, occurs outside of what Marilyn R. Farwell refers to as "the controlling realm of male desire" (100), one may begin to theorize the possibility of lesbian existence in the social sphere as well as a lesbian narrative space in writing about the Holocaust, which persists despite discourses both dominant (nazi juridical discourses, mainstream Holocaust studies resistant to serious treatment of gay men and lesbians as Holocaust victims) and oppositional (some feminist and other radical work in Holocaust studies that does not fully address lesbian existence as a viable lens of Holocaust inquiry) that have attempted to elide it.

The nazis, bolstered by received medical and sociological knowledge at the time, assumed that homosexuality was more widespread among men and less conspicuous in women. The same argument was employed in the United States during World War II and the postwar years, but the historical work of Lillian Faderman and others suggests that the perceived social invisibility was not the result of a small lesbian population, but the "discreet" styles of many lesbians who escaped notice by the heterosexual world (Faderman 185–86). The notion of discretion, including heterosexual marriage as a way of masquerading lesbian desire, is certainly evident in the testimony of Elisabeth Zimmermann just cited, and social conformity as a strategy of survival during the years of nazi rule is certainly evident in many of the life stories Schoppmann collected. Given that lesbian sex was not specifically mentioned in the Reich Penal Code, how might lesbian existence be more specifically theorized? How did lesbian existence, understood as broadly and as socially situated as possible, create a possible social space that challenged the Third Reich's relegation of women to passive sexual roles, tied narrowly to marriage, procreation, and to the institution of heterosexuality in general, and what were the concomitant dangers and, in some cases, actual consequences? Moreover, how can the historical fact of lesbian existence under National Socialism, and in early twentieth-century Germany in general, help create new narrative spaces in Holocaust research and in German cultural history?

Though Paragraph 175 did not criminalize lesbian sexuality, historical records indicate that some nazi jurists did advocate strongly for its inclusion. The reasons as to whether or not to include it provide further insight into nazi gender and sexual politics and show both how lesbians could have been endangered and how their absence from within the juridical code enabled the production of sites of resistance, in varying degrees, to the rigidity of prescribed gender and sexual norms for women under National Socialism. An analysis of arguments for including lesbian sex in the penal code also points to the threat, felt by various nazi individuals and nazi organizations, posed by lesbian existence. A transcript from the minutes of discussions by the Subcommittee of the Committee on Population Policy in March 1936 shows that nazi officials argued the extent to which homosexuality, particularly if it were deemed to be innate, should be considered in terms of the threat it imposed to nazi population policy. The subcommittee believed that population policy was not sufficiently threatened by female homosexuality so as to warrant proposals for its criminalization to be sent to the Criminal Law Commission, under the assumption that if a woman were seduced by another woman, she would not necessarily withdraw from "normal" sexual relations, and could still be "useful" in terms of population growth and development (Minutes of Subcommittee of the Committee on Population Policy, March 2, 1936; in Grau, *Hidden Holocaust?* 71–72). In addition, the subcommittee argued that penal sanctions were difficult to impose on women accused of illicit sex with other women because of a woman's "natural inclination toward effusiveness and caressing" (Minutes of Subcommittee, in Grau, *Hidden Holocaust?* 72), which would make proving the charge difficult. Moreover, as R. Amy Elman notes, lesbians (in one of few similarities to gay men) were not as readily identifiable in that they didn't have the same kind of recognized institutional and social affiliations and birth certification of social stature as did Jews and other racially categorized groups (12).

Other nazi jurists did put forth strong arguments for criminalizing lesbian sex. In arguing for equality between the sexes and for women "as bearers and protectors of the life of the *Volk*," People's Court Justice Ernst Jenne interestingly supported Paragraph 175 of the penal code being extended to women (Jenne, in *Deutsches Recht*, 1936, 469; qtd. in Grau, *Hidden Holocaust?* 78). Concerned that female homosexuality was coming more and more into social view, especially in the larger cities, and that the effects of lesbianism on the morality of national and family life would be the same as "unnatural sex acts between men," Jenne cites Eberhard's book *Feminismus und Kulturuntergang* (1927) to claim a correlation between the absence in the punishability of lesbian sex and the rising influence of women's emancipation and tribadism (Jenne, in *Deutsches Recht*, 1936, 469–70; cited/qtd. in Grau, *Hidden Holocaust?* 78–79). Also Rudolf Klare, in his thesis "Homosexuality and Criminal Law," which was published in 1937, supported the criminalization of lesbian sex by arguing that lesbians bore the same threat of racial degeneration to the Aryan Nation (Schoppmann, "The Campaign Against Homosexuality" 4). However, there were a number of cases where women were prosecuted as lesbian (that is, for example, for abusing relations of dependence based on employment or service, or for explicitly rejecting the sexual advances of senior male military officers to whom they reported and being subjected, as a result, to charges of subversion of military potential).[8] In addition, as Claudia Schoppmann points out, lesbians suffered the destruction of their clubs, the banning of their newsletters, and the close surveillance of bars where they met (Schoppmann, "The Position of Lesbian Women in the Nazi Period" 13); as a result, their sense of public community was destroyed. As Elman notes, the nazis, through the S.A. (*Sturmabteilung* or storm troopers), relied more on intimidation than on actual legislation to oppose a lesbian presence under National Socialism (10). But the final juridical decision regarding the prosecution of lesbians is evident in a letter dated June 18, 1942, from the Reich Minister of Justice to the Reichskommissar for the occupied Norwegian territories in Oslo. The letter specifically stated:

> Homosexual activity between women, apart from prostitutes, is not so widespread as it is among men and, given the more intense manners of social intercourse between women, it more readily escapes public notice. The greater resulting difficulty of establishing such behavior would involve the danger of unfounded testimony and investigations. One major reason for punishing sex offences between men—namely, the distortion of public life by the development of personal ties of dependence—does not apply in the case of women because of their lesser position in state and public employment. Finally, women who indulge in unnatural sexual relations are not lost for ever as procreative factors in the same way that homosexual men are, for experience shows that they later often resume normal relations. (Letter from the Reich Minister of Justice, dated June 18, 1942, Berlin; qtd. in Grau, *Hidden Holocaust?* 84)[9]

But the historical record, and particularly Paragraph 175, should not blind us to the less overt ways (in addition to official prosecutions) lesbians were persecuted, opposed, and silenced under nazi rule. More erroneously, one should not be led to assume that the signifier "homosexuality" under the Third Reich, and in historical research, is reducible to, or conflated with, gay men alone. In addition to the lesbian subcultures in major German cities from the beginning of the twentieth century, which reached a height of visibility and cultural influence and viability under the Weimar, in addition to the exclusion of lesbian sex from the Reich Penal Code, and in addition to a relatively small number of actual prosecutions of women as lesbians, theorizing lesbian existence must involve careful and considered acts of (re)reading against the grain of heteronormativity; that is, as Elman explains it, a reading "between the lines" of memoirs, testimonies, and historical records so as to question carefully automatic presumptions of heterosexuality (10).

Examining carefully the possibilities and specificities of lesbian existence is both a feminist and a lesbian issue as we learn more about nazi power and about women's strategies for resistance and survival. As Ringelheim notes, women's relationships with other women were significantly different from those of men with other men ("The Unethical and the Unspeakable" 81) and therefore must include women's felt connections to other women, whether or not such relationships constituted an erotic component. At the same time, it is problematic to address lesbian existence solely under the rubric of homosexuality, as often occurs in Holocaust research (though sometimes it can be if it is made clear that homosexuality is not reducible to gay men only). Yet the mere conflation of lesbians with gay men privileges sexuality at the expense of gender difference and at the expense of obscuring the affectional non-erotic bonds shared among women. Elman points to the immediate materiality of the problem in searching the archives at the U.S. Holocaust Memorial Museum in Washington, D.C. She notes that search commands on the computers at the USHMM for "lesbian" release mostly information on gay men, as if the pink triangle and Paragraph 175 applied to both groups equally (14). But since the forms of juridical law and actual prosecutions greatly varied for gay men as opposed to lesbians, lesbian existence under National Socialism must be given separate analysis.

One way of theorizing lesbian existence is to point to the fact that what lesbians and many other women resisted was the nazi enforcement of rigid gender norms, especially since, as Robert Proctor notes in *Racial Hygiene*, the nazis saw women as reproductive rather than as political beings, and this was set in legal doctrine (123). For women not already endangered by ethnicity, race, physical or mental handicap, party membership, or political beliefs, the nazis saw Aryan women as predestined for motherhood and the domestic sphere, and therefore as subordinate to men.[10] This gender-specific division of labor was tied to nazi population policy, which aimed to raise the birthrate, which had declined in the period from the early twentieth century to 1932. Proctor notes that in 1900, the German birth rate was thirty-six births per thousand people, whereas by 1932 it had plummeted to fewer than fifteen births per one thousand (124).[11] Along these lines, women were excluded from influential professional careers and from the public sphere of social and political life, and strict quotas were maintained for the admission of female students to German universities. In fact, according to Jonathan Friedman, the nazis lured working women back into the home and offered loans to married men if their wives would stop working, and the principal of the loan could be reduced by one-quarter for each Aryan child born (15).[12]

The consequences of nazi population policy for lesbians who were otherwise not endangered could be quite perilous. Speaking more directly against lesbians, an issue of *Das Schwarze Korps*, an official journal of the SS (*Schutzstaffeln* or elite nazi corps of guard detachments) mentioned in the previous chapter, also spoke about lesbians, indicating that "the true woman" suffers if unmarried, "not because she lacks sexual intercourse, but because she lacks a child and has not answered her calling to motherhood" (*Das Schwarze Korps*, October 21, 1937; qtd. in Schoppmann, *Days of Masquerade* 12). In the case of women, at least within the specificity of juridical discourse, non-heteronormative, non-procreative forms of sexuality were erased, whereas between men, sexual intercourse or intercourse-like acts were specifically encoded into penal law. But since childless marriages were subject to attack and to penalty tax, lesbians, as Schoppmann notes, were more often targets of propaganda against childless and unmarried women, since they usually remained unmarried more often than their heterosexual counterparts (*Days of Masquerade* 12). In addition, the reproach of "masculinization" was often used as a threat to intimidate women who dared to break out of traditional gender norms and the heterosexist social structures that were thought to promote and maintain the stability of the regime (Schoppmann, "The Position of Lesbian Women" 10–11). Signs of overt masculinization could include clothing, hairstyle, or outward behavior, and were a way of policing women's gender roles—and also, less overtly, their sexuality and erotic lives. The link of gender enforcement to population policy, and to the racialization of sexuality discussed in chapter 2, is further evident, then, in the social anxiety prompted by masculine identification in women. A handbook published by a nazi women's organization in 1934 interpreted masculine identification in women as "degenerative signs of a foreign race, which are hostile to procreation and thus destructive to the people. Healthy races do not artificially blur the differences between the sexes" (qtd. in Schoppmann, *Days of Masquerade* 18).[13]

The enforcement of gender norms and heteronormative sexuality placed lesbians in danger if they did not conform to nazi ideals of femininity, which included marriage and motherhood. Claudia Schoppmann's reflection on the lived experience of Elisabeth Zimmermann under the nazis shows that the gender-specific socialization of girls and young women centered on the obligation to be sexually passive and remain chaste, so much so that the process of discovering one's lesbian desires could be spread out over a much longer period of time than was usually the case for gay men. This was true under the Weimar as well, unless young women had access to the lesbian subcultures of the major cities, and sexual passivity *as* conventional femininity was a consistent ideology of feminine gender under the principles of nazi socialization for girls—"*rein bleiben and und reif werden!*" (to remain pure and to mature) (Schoppmann, *Days of Masquerade* 116–17). As a result, many lesbians "masqueraded" or, more accurately, "performed" conventional femininity as a way of appearing to conform to the feminine ideal as a deliberate strategy for remaining inconspicuous.

The internalization and embodiment of norms of Aryan femininity as a way of escaping surveillance and detection as a lesbian, whether through outward appearance and manner in the public sphere—and for some, crossing into the private sphere through renounced relationships with other women and hiding under the pretense of heterosexual marriage and childbearing—were, of course, not an option for women who were racially endangered (Jews, Roma, Sinti), handicapped, or politically endangered for their outspoken political beliefs or overt political actions in ways that were perceived as threatening to the nazi regime. The exception might be a small number of women, whether or not they were lesbian, who might have been able to otherwise hide successfully their Semitic or non-Aryan origins but risk graver persecution if discovered. Yet it must be said that the various forms of masquerade were oppressive to those women who did identify as lesbian, because the masquerade itself undermined self-determination and erotic autonomy, helped diminish the social visibility of lesbians under National Socialism, and enabled little opportunity for lesbians to identify with other women, who might have also been lesbian, for support.

At the same time, the fact that many lesbians could, and often did, remain inconspicuous did not necessarily exempt them from actual persecution or from the fear of possible persecution. While nazi jurists decided not to criminalize lesbian sex in the Reich Penal Code in Germany, Paragraph 129 I-b of the Austrian penal code criminalized all forms of same-sex sexuality, and violators could potentially have received one to five years imprisonment. According to Matti Bunzl, the execution of Paragraph 129 I-b was adapted to the German Paragraph 175 after the country's

Anschluss to nazi Germany in 1938, resulting in intensified prosecutions, countless deportations to concentration camps, and numerous deaths; moreover, Paragraph 129 I-b remained on the books when Austria's Second Republic was constituted after the war (61). While the law criminalized same-sex sexuality regardless of gender, the actual execution of the law mainly concerned men as indicated by criminal statistics (Bunzl 62). But, as with nazi Germany, one cannot assume that lesbians were not endangered or persecuted simply because many were not specifically prosecuted as lesbians according to charges listed in court records. Schoppmann points out that fewer women were charged under Paragraph 129 I-b in Austria because they often met other women privately in homes, whereas gay men tended to meet in more public places ("The Campaign Against Homosexuality" 4), thus creating a sense of immediacy to homosexuality's so-called degenerative effects on the population.

Most important, however—and coming back to my earlier point about not losing sight of the axis of gender—most lesbians were not prosecuted as lesbians but as "asocials." This was a broad, diverse category comprised of those the nazis considered to be socially maladjusted but who had not necessarily committed any offense and were not considered to be members of an "inferior" race. This included prostitutes, thieves, vagrants, those who violated laws prohibiting sexual contact between Aryans and Jews, and resistant women (who failed to live up to the social demands of the nazi totalitarian state regarding, for example, nazi demographic goals, many of whom were lesbian).[14] Yet, as Elman clarifies, the heterogeneity of this group, identified with a black triangle, makes it very difficult to render lesbians legible, along with the fact that lesbians were not as readily identifiable as were other victims of nazi power, even by comparison with gay men, whose pink triangle exclusively signified their "crime" (11). In addition, as Gellately and Stoltzfus observe, to be labeled as asocial was often vaguely and arbitrarily defined in terms of the failure to live up to what the nazis considered to be good citizenship and the fulfillment of one's social obligations (12). For lesbians, this could mean the refusal to stop working, the resistance to heterosexual marriage, the failure to bear children, and, in some cases, simply having affective and erotic ties to other women and refusing to be defined by any relation to men, which, despite the absence of criminalization in nazi Germany, did place many women under threat, and did, in fact, result in more direct forms of persecution in addition to intimidation as ways of opposing lesbian existence.

For example, discussions among some nazi jurists concerning the place of lesbian sex within the law did provoke fear among lesbians, and even among women who simply shared close friendships, that they might be liable to harassment, persecution, or possibly arrest. Anneliese W. (aka Johnny), interviewed by Schoppmann in 1987, mentions the growing climate of fear at the time and how many of her lesbian friends changed their appearance and even married to avoid detection and become less vulnerable. She notes:

> From the very beginning of the Hitler regime, I still kept my short, man's haircut; back then we didn't wear pants anyway, but I had a tailored suit. You can't imagine what people said to us, "Take a look at the gay broads!" and things like that. It was pretty bad. They said it was supposed to be made illegal for women too; it was already illegal for men. (Schoppmann, *Days of Masquerade* 44)

At the same time, fear of the threat of persecution, along with juridical practices already in place that criminalized male homosexuality, cannot overshadow the fact that many women who were lesbian and resisted the gender, sexual, reproductive, and—by implication—the political imperatives of the nazi regime were in fact sent to concentration camps. Anneliese ("Johnny") recalls being with a lover, Helene Bartelt, who had spent two years (1940–42) in Ravensbrück, shortly after her release:

> I was together with her after she was released, not long—maybe a year. She was a very beautiful woman, delicate, blond, and very good-looking. They wanted her to produce munitions as compulsory service and she just said, "That fucking Hitler can make his own munitions." She was arrested for saying that! They picked her up at five in the morning and took her to Ravensbrück. There were many like us in the camp, but whether they were like that before or got that way from being locked up together…? She didn't talk about it much. She wasn't supposed to and was always afraid. Not until we had been together for quite a while did she tell me that she had been abused. They had knocked out her teeth and she had two holes in her head. Later she became a *kapo* and assisted the camp warden, and then she was treated better. She was released after two years for good conduct. She wasn't able to find any work since it was written on her identification papers; that happened a lot. Then, when we broke up, she married a Dane—maybe just to have a place to go, who knows? But that didn't last very long. (Schoppmann, *Days of Masquerade* 52)

Furthermore, even if women were extremely careful, appeared to conform socially, and remained inconspicuous in order to survive in an environment hostile to lesbian existence, one could be denounced as lesbian based on "reasonable suspicion," which could lead to arrest and other consequences. The conditions for denunciations were set up and made possible not only by the authoritarian rule of the nazis, but also by the publicizing of the changes made to the Reich Penal Code concerning homosexuality, nazi population/demographic propaganda (which cast homosexuals as "enemies of the State"), the visible terror of the Röhm purge within the public domain, and appeals to traditional notions of bourgeois respectability as discussed in the previous chapter. While juridical discourses and the practices of persecution that resulted were mainly centered on gay men, lesbians were often linked by implication as enemies of the state. Denunciations could also be used against political opponents as a way of seeking vengeance or simply as a way of gaining status and recognition by the nazi elite. Stefan Micheler rightly claims that those denounced for homosexuality were mostly men but acknowledges that some of those denounced for it were women (122). Again, just because sexual contact between women was not specifically written into law, this did not prevent the pathologization and prosecution of lesbian sex by nazi officials for its perceived threat to population policy, which was the main catalyst for criminalizing male homosexuality. Even though Ellen E. (a twenty-year-old sales representative) and Paul-Reimer I (a painter) pretended to live as a heterosexual couple (as tenants with the family of a dentist in Hamburg) and were engaged to be married in hopes of concealing their same-sex desires, Micheler cites an anonymous letter of denunciation sent to the criminal police, which also cites masculinization as the mark of lesbian visibility:

> You should conduct a raid…on E's love nest. This is the residence of a "mannish woman" who often invites her "own kind," sometimes more than just one, into her lodgings. In times like these, we clearly should not tolerate such §175 activities (à la Röhm). Since there are children living in the house, immediate action must be taken. Obviously, it is inadvisable for our youth to observe such activities. (Anonymous letter to criminal police, dated April 28, 1941, Rep. 6776/41; qtd. in Micheler 122–23)

Micheler notes that Paul-Reimer I was sentenced to eight months in prison and that the prosecutor and the court also imposed voluntary castration (which Paul-Reimer underwent), while the fate of Ellen E. is not known (123).

Another example of enforced masquerade was through the psychic violence of being forced to deny one's affectional bonds altogether. In 1944, Elisabeth (Lily) Wust, who was the wife of a nazi officer, underwent torturous interrogation to force her to deny that she had had sexual relations with Felice Schragenheim. Schragenheim was a Jewish woman who was initially arrested as an "asocial" in 1941 and then re-arrested by the Gestapo as a Jew after living underground. She died in Bergen-Belsen in 1945 (Elman 15n). According to Elman, admission of a sexual liaison with another woman would have meant internment in a concentration camp; Wust admitted to no lesbian love between her and Schragenheim, and the recorded lie lasted for decades. In 1991, Wust set the record straight, so to speak, ending decades of agonizing silence by telling her story to American journalist Erica Fischer (Elman 10–11), who published *Aimée & Jaguar* in 1995. The book is based on the lives of Wust and Schragenheim and was later made into a film of the same title.[15]

To assume, then, that lesbians were not systematically persecuted is a difficult premise to support, because the criminalization of male homosexuality (and the nazi propaganda that villainized it) often created similar anxieties about lesbian existence and the fear of potential danger among lesbians themselves, especially in light of nazi population politics and the attendant gender norms to which women were expected to conform for the good of the race and the nation. At the same time, there is evidence that lesbians were also put to work as prostitutes in concentration camp brothels. Else (surname unknown) was originally sent to Ravensbrück as an "asocial," most likely because she was lesbian. Under circumstances still unclear—the historical record is rather sketchy—Else was then sent to the Flossenbürg camp, mostly containing prisoners who were male "asocials" and "criminals." Many female prisoners were often forced to work in camp brothels for a period of "service," and the nazis thought that if such female prisoners were lesbian "it would shape them up" (Schoppmann, *Days of Masquerade* 21).[16] Similarly, a report on a Luftwaffe assistant deported to a concentration camp for rejecting the sexual advances of a nazi officer and arrested by the secret military police for subversion of military potential, as mentioned earlier, notes that at the Bützow camp where she was interred, lesbians were kept in a separate block from men and from other women. The SS guards set the interned Russian and French prisoners of war on the imprisoned lesbians and told them to "fuck them up good and proper" (Grau, Report on a Luftwaffe assistant deported to a concentration camp, *Hidden Holocaust?* 82–83).[17]

More research on the status of lesbians under the Third Reich remains to be done within the larger parameters of feminist work on the nazi period so that the historical fact of lesbian existence and the persecution of lesbians under the Third Reich can be more clearly portrayed and understood within Holocaust scholarship. What we do know about lesbians and women who resisted the gender norms and population policies enforced under nazi rule should enable more critical (re)readings of historical documents and texts from the period so as to deconstruct what Marilyn Farwell has referred to as the bond between heterosexuality and narrative (102). One obvious place to begin is to question lesbian desire as the consequence of dire circumstances under which many women became close in the camps. Certainly there is some truth to this; Ringelheim notes, for instance, that women did construct survival strategies and make meaningful choices under varying conditions of powerlessness ("The Unethical and the Unspeakable" 81). One such strategy for survival might have been, for some women, deep friendships and social networks with other women, with or without an erotic component, which could be conceived as one possible space of lesbian existence. But Ringelheim does caution that some women's testimonies have fallen on deaf ears; this is especially the case where desires for other women are explicit and obviously not the result of enforced, closed confinement or loneliness alone. In studying Holocaust victims, we need to understand the wider variety of material conditions and social relations through which certain groups, such as women, (re)created "families" and other networks of survival (Ringelheim 80). The re-creation of families and affectional bonds is often a necessary trajectory for lesbians (and for gay men) and has often been crucial to queer survival both under oppressive conditions and in the material realities of everyday life in what is still, at times, a hostile social world. These strategies of survival, then, need to be meaningfully woven into dominant narratives of Holocaust scholarship rather than simply being confined to a singular, circumstantial form of lesbian sexuality within the confines of the ghettos or the camps.

Turning the tables to examine heterosexuality, which simply passes as un(re)marked in much Holocaust scholarship, might we ask whether heterosexual desire could be similarly dismissed as a momentary aberration, resulting from the circumstances of close confinement? But the idea is not as far-fetched as one may initially believe; Elman convincingly argues that if we can argue for heterosexuality as the result of circumstance and separation from the rest of the world, our memory of Anne Frank could be considerably altered. The possibilities of a lesbian narrative space might very well exist in the pages of Anne Frank's famous diary if we examine it carefully and read it against the grain of heteronarrativity:

> I already had these kinds of feelings subconsciously before I came here, because I remember that once when I slept with a girl friend I had a strong desire to kiss her, and that I did do so. I could not help being terribly inquisitive over her body, for she had always kept it hidden from me. I asked her whether, as proof of our friendship, we should feel one another's breasts, but she refused. I go into ecstasies every time I see the naked figure of a woman, such as Venus, for example. It strikes me as so wonderful and exquisite that I have difficulty in stopping the tears rolling down my cheeks.
>
> If only I had a girl friend!
>
> Yours, Anne (*Anne Frank: The Diary of a Young Girl* 117; qtd. in Elman 14)

Given the brutal honesty and passion with which this diary entry is written, there is more to it, I believe, than what might be easily dismissed as adolescent curiosity and experimentation. As more time passes in the hideaway annex, Anne becomes friends with, and attracted to, Peter van Daan. Yet, as Elman points out, Anne's relation to Peter is hardly discussed as a schoolgirl's crush exacerbated by desperate living conditions and the absence of female companionship! Rather, Anne "lived and died in a world similar to our own, a world that presumed she was (and would be) straight" (Elman 14–15).[18]

Lesbian existence remains to be more credibly enfolded into Holocaust research, but this cannot be accomplished by traditional historical approaches that rely on hard archival and textual evidence alone. Research needs to build further on what we do know about lesbian existence in order to postulate its possibility rather than denying it because it does not seem to appear in historical documents in visible form and can be easily overlooked. We do know, as I have shown in this chapter, and as other work has demonstrated aptly, that a vibrant lesbian subculture existed under the Weimar in Berlin and in other major German cities. But it would be reductive to then assume that homophobic reaction to lesbian and gay visibility under the Weimar was completely absent. Likewise, under the heightened homophobic panic of nazism, it would be similarly reductive to assume that lesbian life ceased to exist (even though the overt lesbian subculture of the Weimar, for the most part, did) as attested by the ongoing presence of gay men (despite the heightening of draconian laws and strategies of persecution against them), and despite the deliberate attempts at the repression of same-sex desire by the nazi state.

How can one assume that lesbian existence was any less significant even if it was not specifically inscribed on the social register? Both lesbians and gay men shared *presence* under National Socialism, but the comparison usually ends there, since lesbian existence cannot be understood under the same rubric as male homosexuality except in limited ways and in isolated examples (the re-creation of families or social networks, both groups being prone to denunciation, both groups not being readily identifiable for their sexuality through identification papers or birth certificates, etc.). For instance, even though lesbians were not criminalized under the Reich Penal Code, discussions among some nazi jurists concerning the legality of lesbian sex did show an awareness of lesbian existence as well as its perceived threat to the Reich's population policy and sense of national cohesion (which formed the basis for the criminalization of male homosexuality). But the comparison breaks down at these junctures, and as I have tried to argue in this chapter, interrogation of the axis of gender, rather than the axis of sexuality alone, which is primarily used in the study of gay men under National Socialism, can help produce new possibilities for theorizing lesbian existence and a lesbian narrative space in Holocaust research. This will also enable better analysis of the ways in which some women labeled as "asocial," and persecuted for their resistance to multiple forms of domination (including fixed gender norms, marriage, procreation, restriction to the domestic sphere, and sexual dominance by nazi officers with whom they might have worked), could quite possibly have been lesbian even though their sexuality may not be immediately apparent in the historical record. Another clue to lesbian existence is the actuality of recorded survival testimony, some of which has been discussed here, which needs to be enfolded more meaningfully into the dominant body of Holocaust research, rather than remaining relegated to the borders, reduced to a footnote, or altogether neglected as a serious strand of inquiry. At the same time, queer studies needs to engage research on lesbians under National Socialism as a way of articulating another mode of lesbian existence within this particular historical period. Challenges to the denial or absence of lesbian existence, or to the specific persecutions of women who were lesbian, will not only broaden the full range of women's experiences under the Third Reich, but will also challenge the heteronormative frames of reference by which we understand the past and the "evidence" we use to formulate that understanding.

4

Homosexuality and Fascism: A (Re)Analysis

Given that same-sex desires pertaining to both lesbians and gay men cannot be situated within National Socialism without an analysis of population and reproductive politics, racial hygiene, and the racialization of sexuality, as well as accounting for the preservation of social respectability tied to, among other things, the social adherence to rigid gender norms, nazi homophobia cannot simply be regarded as a form of oppression in and of itself, dehistoricized and decontextualized from other strategies of power. At the same time, nazi fascism was not only made manifest through the more visible exercise and deployment of political might (storm troopers, persecutions, deportations, euthanasia, medical experimentation, mass executions, extermination), but also through the careful and deliberate discursive construction of the nation as heterosexual, as well as carefully crafted narratives of national belonging and appeals to an idealized, mythological past. European nationalism, enhanced in many respects by scientific racism, eugenics, and theories of evolution and genealogy, provided a discursive system of inscription for fascist ideology and a new way of conceiving of the nation-state. As George Mosse notes, fascism was, in many respects, a *nationalist* revolution with its own ideologies and goals, where the citizenry was "transformed from spectators to participants" (*Fascist Revolution* xi–xii).

One general feature of nationalism, more evident, perhaps, in postcolonial nationalisms through ongoing attempts over the past fifty to sixty years at national (re)building in the period following colonial occupation and rule, is the preservation of the sanctity of the inner core of national culture (indigenous language[s], particular traditions that have withstood the test of time, cultural history, mythologies, etc.), which must be protected, at all costs, from foreign intrusion.¹ In discussing postcolonial nationalisms, Partha Chatterjee notes that they are not a mere mimicry of European nationalisms as Benedict Anderson contends.² Rather, they are based on their difference from the forms of nationalism propagated by the West through the imitation of western skills and technologies in order to develop the material domain of the nation, and the simultaneous and deliberate struggle to preserve the distinctiveness of the spiritual aspect of national culture which must be protected from western encroachment (*Nation and Its Fragments* 5–6). Unlike postcolonial nationalisms, whereby an alien (western) culture has to be adapted to reach global standards of progress set by the West, which are defined in terms of promoting the social interests of the West and perpetuating global relations of power (Chatterjee, *Nationalist Thought* 14), along with an inner domain of sovereignty and trace of cultural authenticity and distinctiveness which must be preserved, western European nationalisms generally have not been characterized by, or bound to, such a splitting. This is because European nations often thought of themselves as already sufficiently equipped from within to meet the standards of progress they set for themselves. Yet the protection of the inner domain of national culture that Chatterjee describes as pertaining to the postcolonial peripheries is not necessarily altogether alien to the construction of national cultures in the western metropolitan centers, especially in terms of what is marked as alien, foreign, or outside the realm of national belonging, and this is particularly salient in the case of National Socialism.

So, while postcolonial nationalisms cannot be reducible to those in Europe, insofar as the "state" preceded the nation through imperial control of the colonies, there is a link to the extent that nationalism in both contexts can provide a foundation for fascism and totalitarian rule insofar as nationalism's ideological framework can be used as a way of marking hyperbolically those outside the boundaries of national belonging. In Germany, National Socialism especially marked Jews, Roma, Sinti, and other non-Aryans, as well as homosexuals (understood within the larger framework of racial and population politics) as other. Similarly, in many nations formerly colonized, homosexuality, feminism, and particular ethnic, linguistic, or religious groups are sometimes in conflict with the thinking of nationalist elites and are read as unwelcome intrusions in the national imaginary. While European nationalism seems very much guided by benign and altruistic concerns for liberty, freedom, sovereignty, and national belonging—having its roots in Enlightenment thinking, as Chatterjee notes—it similarly justified the brutality of nazism, was part of the ideology of racial hatred in the colonies, and has given rise to mindless chauvinism and xenophobia and the justification of organized violence and tyranny (*Nationalist Thought* 2) by maintaining a strict demarcation between self (those who constitute and are constituted by the nation) and other.

While I have discussed the racialization of homosexuality and the enforcement of rigid regimes of gender in relation to Third Reich population politics and theories of racial degeneracy, which set up certain groups of people as enemies of the nazi state, I wish to explore further the chauvinism, xenophobia, and violence mentioned by Chatterjee. I will do so by examining more closely the relationship between fascist power under National Socialism and its rhetoric of nationalism, specifically its rather contradictory appeals to masculinity and homoeroticism, and question the mere conflation of fascism with homosexuality as a way of understanding nazi power.

Arguably, the brutality of nationalism under the Third Reich and its attendant xenophobia and tyranny is not unrelated to its frantic preoccupation with masculinity and/as power. Some scholars have argued that the cult of phallic masculinity surrounding fascism, portrayed in its nationalist images, forms a link in German cultural history to the homosocial bonds between men, specifically to the *Männerbund* tradition, which can be traced back to romantic friendships between men in eighteenth-century Germany and reappeared as a variation in the late nineteenth and early twentieth centuries as the *Gemeinschaft der Eigenen*. The *Männerbund* tradition is important because it symbolized devotion to physical strength and devotion to masculinity and male comradeship and provided a recognized social space wherein men could prove their manliness to themselves and to each other.[3] The other link of male homosociality and nazi power, according to Mosse, comes from the experience of World War I, derived from the model of the frontline male soldier leading the charge against the enemy, which transformed the soldier into a stereotype (*Nationalism and Sexuality* 154–55), as captured in the image of the nazi storm trooper, and which continued the quest for war and contempt for the enemy outsider, cast as feminine. Both the historical precedence of the *Männerbund* and the experience of war enabled a nostalgia for male comradeship. The glorification of struggle, represented by the horrors of war, mass death, and wounded and mutilated enemies and comrades, provided an escape from the banalities of everyday life; male comradeship and soldiering were also seen by many men as a way of resisting class divisions within the nation (Mosse, *Fascist Revolution* 15; 17–18). The impact of war, and the concomitant violence that surrounded it for frontline soldiers who survived, served the purposes of fascism later on, not only through a reinscription of masculine comradeship experienced in the trenches, but later through the immunity to pain and indifference to suffering at the hands of male leaders in the ranks of nazi power, and the simultaneous struggle for masculinity within the nation-state through ridding itself of its enemies who would weaken the nation and its place in the world.

Given the bonds between men that developed during wartime and in the *Männerbund* tradition and its variations, the cult of phallic masculinity that developed in the early twentieth century (such as in German fraternity and gymnastic societies) very much exemplified the masculine Nietzschean stereotype of physical strength and invulnerability, an ideal by which men compared their own masculinity. The new fascist man that emerged under nazi fascism was, according to Mosse, physically strong, courageous, and spartan, that is, in control of his passions, sacrificing them for the greater good of the nation (*Fascist Revolution* 30–31). Yet the worship of masculinity, and the longing for it, not only had appeal to gay men, as Mosse suggests in discussing the seduction of some French homosexuals to the masculine aura of the nazis and their collaboration with the nazis under the German Occupation of France, but, more broadly, was informed by homoeroticism, which had also played a role in male camaraderie in wartime and in the *Männerbund* tradition, and possibly explains, on some level, the wider appeal of fascist power (*Fascist Revolution* 181). In a sense, the attraction to the homoerotic within fascism is an attraction to both power and transgression, whereby homoeroticism, as Klaus Theweleit has observed, was encoded and even intimately felt, but never publicly expressed or acknowledged. Instead, it was codified and simultaneously displaced as a defiant escape from the restrictions of bourgeois morality, as transgression, as boyish mischief, as a perverse performance or acting out, or as an act of terror against other men (323). In other words, the pleasure of male bonding under nazi fascism was an act prescribed and structured by the social order, an act of reterritorialization based on the eroticization of power (and the disavowal of that eroticization) over other men (Theweleit 325). Its reterritorialization, however, pertains predominately to the social sphere as centered, unified, easily identifiable, and contained by the powerful elite cadre of males who constituted the power center of the national imaginary and appropriated its definable characteristics as masculine and as a repudiation of the feminine (chaos, fragmentation, disorder) as embodied by those marked on the constitutive outside of formative discourses of national belonging.[4] Nazi struggles for masculinity are thus struggles for men to become men as Theweleit notes (82) but are similarly struggles to repudiate femininity both within themselves and within the nation-state, hence a regime of totalitarian rule and the simultaneous need for the erasure of social difference.

But rather than a rejection of femininity, others have argued that hypermasculine fascist power might simply be a displacement of femininity, and, by analogy, of homosexuality. Citing Theodor Adorno's *Minima Moralia*, Andrew Hewitt has suggested that hypermasculinity is really a form of effeminacy arranged around the axiom of sexual power; that is, homosexuality is an act of estrangement, "a mirror in which heterosexual relations confront and displace themselves" (Hewitt, *Political Inversions* 55–56). This means that homosexuality, or at least a latent homoeroticism, could be the underlying structure for fascist relations of rule as attempts are, at the same time, constantly and insistently proffered to disavow homosexual desire, expression, or attachment. Along these lines, homosexuality, according to Hewitt, is always already performative, acting itself out, or masquerading as heterosexuality, representing not only the repression of desire, but desire as/for repression (*Political Inversions* 57). Speaking of the hypermasculinity of "he-men" in positions of power in totalitarian regimes, Adorno states in *Minima Moralia*, mostly written during World War II, that totalitarianism and homosexuality are linked to the extent that the subject of the "he-man," through gestures of virility and self-assuredness of his power to rule and command, constitutes, in effect, a site of skepticism rather than one of surety and certainty. At the fantasmatic foundation of he-men's masculinity and projected symbolic virility is a lie; the so-called "tough guys" within a totalitarian regime, according to Adorno, are really effeminate and need those who are weak or disempowered as their victims so as to prove that they are not similar to them. As agents of repression, as sadists, however, tough guys repress their own homosexuality, performing repressed homosexuality as the only approved form of heterosexuality (Adorno 45–46).[5]

Under fascism, masculine privilege is sustained by male homosocial bonding, male fraternity, and a repudiation of feminine identifications. Yet, at the same time, nazi hypermasculinity, through its necessary homosocial bonds and homoerotic potentialities—especially through the eroticization of the power of men over men—placed nazi masculinity into crisis, calling into question a firm demarcation between the borders of hetero- and homosexuality. The same erotic fantasies of subordination of men by men were also evident under colonialism. Edward Said and others have noted that orientalism produced an occidental mode of perception whereby the West projected an aberrant sexual otherness, that is, "a different type of sexuality," onto the East (Said 190). This act of appropriation, occurring in the contact zone between imperial power and indigenous sexualities, both mirrored the psychosexual needs of the West and, in the process, justified colonial domination and helped fulfill its civilizing mission. But as Hema Chari further argues in elaborating the heterosexist slant in Said's claim, colonial power sustained imperial domination by also appropriating an ambivalent, yet systematic, process of avowal and disavowal of sexual desire between men; that is, the ambivalence of colonialist masculine erotics, and the discursive deferral and displacement of homoeroticism, underwrote colonial power (279). While postcolonial work does not necessarily regard colonial masculinity as a form of repressed homosexuality in the same way I have been describing nazi performativities of hypermasculinity in Adorno, the ambivalent avowal of, and simultaneous distancing from, sexual desire between men in the ranks of power, the arousal and displacement of homoeroticism, interpellation by the demands of compulsory heterosexuality, and the fear of feminine threats to masculine power and empire, did seem to underwrite and sustain homosocial relations of rule in both domains.

But is fascism, then, "pathologized" gender to the extent that nazi hypermasculinity was possibly a compensation for the repression of femininity that must not have been sufficiently repressed as it should have been and thereby hindered the development of fully achieved masculine gender identity and, therefore, heterosexuality? Certainly, on some level, it may seem feasible to account for nazi fascism's "queer" moments, given the cultural and historical connections of its homosocial bonds to German cultural history and to the male fraternity experienced by German soldiers during World War I, though certainly not all of the men who were in the military at the time became nazis or had fascist leanings. The connections of nazi fascist power to phallic masculinity were also apparent in German nationalism's configuration of the nation as masculine, powerful, and containing within its borders a unified superior race, in the homoeroticism engendered by nazi hypermasculinity both within the nazi ranks and as read by the German *Volk* and those colonized in the occupied territories, and in the conflation of the two with absolute power of men over other men. Theoretically, the connections of nazism to hypermasculinity, homosociality, and homoeroticism lend themselves to a psychoanalytic understanding of masculinity as a misogynistic fear of, and flight from, femininity through unconscious associations of femininity with castration (and, symbolically, with the fear of loss of power and stable ego boundaries which threaten reabsorption and regression to a non-differentiated state that existed previously in the infant's pre-oedipal relation with the mother). Politically, this could be used, as it has been in Theweleit's work, to expose the nazi worship of masculinity and the male Aryan body (a gender identity achieved through violent forms of separation to achieve masculine gender identity) as well as the hypocrisy of the regime in its persecution of gay men. More important, however, the ideology of masculine superiority and power could also be symptomatic of a fear of the threat of women's power, particularly that of lesbians and other women who resisted nazi gender ideologies, and could widen the scope of inquiry around sexuality, gender, and power, since lesbians and/as resistant women would represent a threat to nazi masculinity so conceived. Indeed, as Melanie Hawthorne and Richard Golsan observe, "given that fascism can be considered the 'ideology of masculine superiority ... and violent rejection of non-subservient or nonidealized women,' ... fascism, it would appear, is in its most basic configuration a masculine—indeed, a pathologically masculine— ideology" (1).[6]

But while fascist power relies on homosocial bonds, it would be erroneous to assume a fantasy of nazi homosexuality. Rather, as Eve Sedgwick has argued, it is more accurate to account for the ways in which German fascism "emerged on a social ground in which 'the homosexual question' had been made highly salient" ("Privilege of Unknowing" 49, n14) through the production of discourses on homosexuality at the time, especially within the juridical and medical spheres of the Third Reich, as I discussed in chapter 2. While I have attempted to account for the masculinist, yet homosocial, bonds that characterized nazi fascism, without dismissing their slipperiness into homoerotic intensification as felt, rather than as necessarily enacted, desire, nazi fascism is double-edged in that it is similarly characterized by a disavowal not of homosocial bonds but of their homoerotic fulfillment. The homosocial space is worth studying not to argue for nazi leaders as repressed or latent homosexuals, or as having a form of gender dysphoria, as indicated by a literal reading of some of Adorno's wartime and postwar writings which reinforce gender dichotomies, but for the ways in which "the homosexual question" became significant under the auspices of National Socialism and was discursively entangled with gender politics and a nexus of other social categories, institutions, and nodes of organization, *which helped register homosexuality discursively in the public sphere*. Simply theorizing a close relation between the intensity of strong homosocial bonds among nazi men and/as homosexuality elides the simultaneous disavowal of felt same-sex desires and the prohibitions against their enactment, and ignores the impact of Hitler's decision in 1941 to denounce the "plague of homosexuality" by prescribing the death penalty for those in the SS and Secret Police convicted under Paragraph of 175 of the Reich Penal Code. This would not, of course, preclude the possibilities of homosexual relations between men in the elite ranks of the Nazi Party from having nonetheless occurred despite such prohibitions (as they certainly did, given the reasoning behind the murder of Ernst Röhm by the SS in 1934 and Hitler's 1941 decision). Yet, it is important to note that such instances of homosexuality within the SS and among other high-ranking nazi men were most likely the exception rather than the rule itself. The homosocial bonds formed within the cadre of men within the Nazi Party are significant, as they formed part of the specific meanings of same-sex bonds, both in terms of their marked saliency under the Third Reich and their social management under powerful strategies of homophobic surveillance, discipline, and regulation. As Sedgwick reminds us, "fascism is distinctive in [the twentieth] century not for the intensity of its homoerotic charge, but rather for the virulence of the homophobic prohibition by which that charge, once crystallized as an object of knowledge, is then denied *to* knowledge and hence most manipulably mobilized" ("Privilege of Unknowing" 50).

Sedgwick's claim is an important one because it would account for the intensity of homosocial bonds and the recognition and disavowal of their homoerotic potential, and because it helps to expose further, I believe, the limitations of a focus purely on the eroticization of nazi power or on the repressed homosexuality of particular high-ranking nazi officials. Such focuses are limiting because they fail to consider, as I have argued throughout this book, the ways in which (homo)sexual desire is not only privately felt, but always already publicly mediated and discursively and historically produced and situated. Similar to my earlier critique of Holocaust scholarship that analyzes homosexuals as subject to nazi persecution because of *what they did*, a mere homosexualization of nazi fascism that attempts to set up a relationship of cause and effect between fascism and homosexuality elides homosexuality as *signifier* within a larger system of signifying practices in relation to other codes, symbols, and cultural meanings.[7] This is particularly the case in light of references to "the homosexual question" in nazi disputes about its criminal status, which are a matter of historical record. Rather than simply conflating homosexuality and/as fascism or vice versa, it is possible to acknowledge, as Hewitt does, that the study of masculinist sexualities can help us to understand, to some extent, the construction of fascism (rather than its "reality"), and that a study of fascism can, in some ways, shed light on the necessity of the creation of strong male homosocial bonds and desires (*Political Inversions* 36), but that is as far as I would be willing to go.

Conflating fascism with homosexuality is also problematic to the extent that it reduces all fascists to repressed homosexuals and locates the source of fascism in homosexuality. There are difficulties with the reductionism of such a move, which would involve either a study of individuals who were both homosexual and fascist (and the sample would be rather small indeed, given the threat of death for homosexual acts committed by men within the nazi leadership), or a theorization of homosexuality among nazi leaders based on their fascist symptoms (which would "predispose" them to homosexuality a priori). But the conflation becomes even more problematic, and highly contestable, within Holocaust scholarship, because those gay men and lesbians who have struggled to be recognized as Holocaust victims are converted from the status of victims, barely secured and recognized as such, and potentially put on nearly the same par as the fascist perpetrators themselves. If homosexuality is once again represented as symptomatic (of fascism, or fascist behaviors as being symptomatic of homosexuality), then "we risk," as Hewitt remarks, "hypostatizing homosexuality as absolutely external to the subject of homophobic social and political discourse" (*Political Inversions* 11). Furthermore, beyond the specific realm of Holocaust studies, such a position is further flawed politically for its pathologization of the other in gendered and sexual terms. Seeing the tough masculine façade of the male fascist as symptomatic of an underlying or latent homosexuality is not rhetorically different from the opposition of sexual virility and potency (as symbolic of the phallic strength of the nation which is coded as a lack in fascist men under such a paradigm) to the (ef) feminization of those deemed to be outside the domain of the national imaginary (who supposedly threaten national strength and cohesion). According to Hewitt, the trope of the weak or effeminate homosexual is evident both in the communist's homosexualization of the fascist as well as in the nazi fascist's effeminization of Jews (*Political Inversions* 9–10). The same gendered oppositions and appropriations of the other as sexually flawed and gender dysphoric still vilify homosexuality in much the same way that oppressive regimes such as fascism and colonialism did. But now they recur under the guise of a critique of such regimes, what Hewitt refers to as forms of "homo-fascism"—a term not referring to individual homosexuals who also happened to be fascist, but to the discursive reduction of homosexuality to fascism, or to the location of homosexuality as fascism's source. More precisely, homo-fascism is the conflation of sexual with political deviance, whereby homosexuality is pathologized as a fascistic fascination with the erotics of power, and fascism is reduced to a psychosexual manifestation of homosexual narcissism, as put forth in some of the psychopolitical writings by the Frankfurt School (Hewitt, *Political Inversions* 39).

Psychoanalytic approaches that try to find a link between fascism and homosexuality, or explain fascism as having its origins in homosexuality, are similarly flawed insofar as they attempt to reduce homosexuality to a discrete identity and to a condition or symptom in opposition to normative heterosexuality, naturally linked to psychic, gender, and sexual stability to the extent that normative masculinity supposedly would not need to repudiate femininity through strategies of displacement, as did nazi fascists through their violent and excessive exercise and deployment of power. Post-Freudian psychoanalysis has not been without its own homo-fascist tendencies. The intent to pathologize nazi fascism as latent or repressed homosexuality works simultaneously as a (re-)pathologization of homosexuality as a disturbed abuse of power. Freud, on the other hand, specifically argued against a causal link between homosexuality and any kind of pathology or degeneracy in his *Three Essays on the Theory of Sexuality* (4), and he especially warned against psychoanalytic attempts to identify or describe homosexuality in psychically discrete terms. He writes:

> Psychoanalytic research is most decidedly opposed to any attempt at separating off homosexuals from the rest of mankind as a group of special character. By studying sexual excitations other than those that are manifestly displayed, it has found that all human beings are capable of making a homosexual object-choice and have in fact made one in their unconscious.... [P]sychoanalysis considers that a choice of an object independently of its sex—freedom to range equally over male and female objects—as it is found in childhood, in primitive states of society and early periods of history, is the original basis from which, as a result of restriction in one direction or the other, both the normal and the inverted types develop. (11–12n)

Despite Freud's problematic use of such terms as "normal" and "invert," the questionable nuances of "primitive states of society" to the extent that these might refer to non-western societies and reify western imperialism, in addition to the subsequent reduction of his work by some to a more or less sweeping bisexual disposition in everyone, Freud's refusal to set up homosexuality as a discrete characteristic or identity is useful socially and politically. It points implicitly to the coercive and oppressive technologies of surveillance and detection to make it culturally intelligible in none other than homophobic terms, a strategy that offers a site of potential discursive redeployment in the conflation of homosexuality with fascism.

My attempt to argue throughout this book that homosexuality under the Third Reich be studied not through essentialist or clinical means, but that it be situated socially and historically, may, of course, seem a rather tired and dated statement to be making at this point in queer studies, well past the thirty plus years since Foucault proposed sexuality to be a historical and cultural invention. But as queer work has begun to move across discrete national borders as the demarcation for studying sexual subjectivities culturally, and even though we have become more attentive to the shifts, to the differences and remainders that refuse to be contained under totalized understandings of sexuality which put further pressure on the reduction of homosexuals to a "type" (which is the legacy of medical and clinical interventions irrespective of Freud), this sort of reduction is precisely what has taken place in the representation of gay men in much historical work on nazism, the Holocaust, and related topics, and certainly in work that posits a causal relation between, or a conflation of, homosexuality and fascism. Foucauldian approaches are important within this particular domain of knowledge production because they question gay desire, or even queerness itself, as reducible to particular bodies, or particular identities, and since they insist that sexualities be analyzed and understood *relationally* within the social field and under a set of specific material, historical, and ideological conditions. As Hewitt argues, what is eroticized is not merely the male object of desire but the homosocial bond on which a patriarchal order depends ("Sleeping with the Enemy" 126); that is, a queering not only of identities with regard to those in nazi power (and those subjected to it), but a more subtle queering of social relations. Psychoanalytically speaking, in cultural rather than in clinical terms, as Hewitt explains, castration is the detachment (or gap) making possible a social and symbolic order by excluding a transcendent signifier from a system of exchange ("Sleeping with the Enemy" 137) insofar as linguistic signification operates as a system of differences as each signifier remains distinct from others. But this principle of difference must also apply to the relation between signifier and signified (that is, for example, between the perceptible quality of a word and its meaning), which is the legacy of Saussurean linguistics. By splitting these two aspects of the verbal sign (signifier and signified), Saussure goes on to argue that all language is a system of relations and differences, and that verbal signs, therefore, do not function through their intrinsic value, but through their differences and their relative position within the signifying system (De Saussure 118). Rather than referring unproblematically and straightforwardly to a plenitude of presence and meaning, the signified must always already function as another signifier, which defers any final transcendent meaning, since signifier and signified never form any relation of absolute congruence because their relationship will always already be fraught with a residue of difference. Given that it is the principle of difference that constitutes language as a signifying system, one signifier both replaces, and, at the same time, *displaces* another, as Jacques Derrida would later propose in taking Saussure further, so that meaning remains endlessly deferred in the movement and play that is signification, creating and sustaining a perpetual gap between signifier and signified, between word and meaning. As Derrida writes: "This reference to the meaning of a signified thinkable and possible outside of all signifiers remains dependent upon the onto-theo-teleology that I have just evoked [the metaphysics of and desire for presence and plenitude of meaning].... That the signified is originally and essentially ... trace, that it is *always already in the position of the signifier*" (73) defers meaning and creates the gap, the residue, the slippage that cannot be contained in the movement from sign to sign.

I mention this because dominant work on fascism and sexuality that attempts to mark men in nazi power as latent homosexuals is flawed to the extent that it (re)creates an essentialized gay identity or prototype without analyzing more closely the blind spots or gaps in such questionable constructions that reattach pathology and failed or abject gender to the signifier "homosexuality." Work that attempts to use Freudian psychoanalysis to conflate nazi fascism with homosexuality does not go far enough in pointing to the fissures between homosexuality as signifier and its variant and shifting meanings at particular historical moments. The same slippages of meaning of which Saussure implied, and Derrida more explicitly theorized as deconstruction, is also taken up in Lacanian psychoanalysis. Lacan not only recognized the perpetual indeterminacies between signifier and signified, but held that all meanings are not available at the conscious level of language, and suggested that unconscious desire can impinge upon language and meaning as well as have its own signifying structure. He speaks of the "incessant sliding of the signified under the signifier" (*Écrits* 154) to argue that the pathway to meaning is never linear or straightforward, and to put pressure on the conception of Cartesian subjectivity, inherited from the Enlightenment in the West, which views all language and thought as the product of a centered, autonomous, and fully conscious mind. Just as a signifier refers not to a self-present meaning, but to other signifiers, and therefore to a displacement or indeterminacy of meaning, the absence, or lack, of what it might substitutively stand for (if there were a one-to-one correspondence between signifier and signified), there is a link to desire which, similarly, shifts from signifier to signifier in the absence of full satisfaction. As Elizabeth Wright has cogently argued, the absence of satisfaction has to be accepted as the unconscious remains in search for the object that has been lost (103). The loss of plenitude, of self-present meaning, psychically the splitting of the primal attachment to the mother, renders desire (for transcendent meaning, for presence, for plenitude) the ongoing effect of all symbolic signification.[8]

I think that Hewitt hints somewhat at the nuances available in Derridean and Lacanian thinking I have been discussing, albeit briefly, as he questions a straightforward, unproblematic conflation of fascism with homosexuality, though his analysis could probably be taken a bit further. If the threat of castration results in the fear of, and flight from, femininity in men, the repression of desire, and the inauguration of a set of detachments (between mother and child, between signifier and signified) that is the condition of the symbolic order, can fellatio, stereotypically a *sine qua non* of homosexual sex (along with anal penetration), undo the castrating gesture or the imagined effects of castration? On one level, fellatio represents the ingestion of the phallus, a metaphor for one man's fellating another man's penis in a gay sexual context or—perhaps on a less literal level—a metaphor for desire for totalitarian authority and order symbolized by the phallus for the fascist (and the ingestion of masculinity and male power for the homosexual), which could superficially link fascism and homosexuality. But such a reading once again attempts to impose a singular transcendent meaning onto the sign of homosexuality (as well as to the phallus) in addition to reading homosexuality symptomatically rather than accounting for its plurality and multiple meanings and its potentialities as a politically resistant position (though it is not always self-evidently resistant). It would be rather naïve to assume that fellatio, symbolically the ingestion of the phallus, undoes not only the threat of castration, but the splittings, separations, and absences that are the forfeitures required by the symbolic, patriarchal order. Nor should one assume that fellatio represents some sort of prelinguistic, preoedipal return to, or a replacement of, narcissistic identification or to fantasies of self-sameness and resemblance that mark all imaginary processes without the mediation of difference(s).[9] Yet, more important, I think, to what is desired is the resultant lack; one must recall that for Lacan, the phallus is not a material, anatomical body part, but the *image* of the penis (*Écrits* 319; emphasis added). More specifically, the phallus "is even less the organ, penis or clitoris, that it symbolizes" (*Écrits* 285). Hence, there is always a gap, a space between the anatomical part and the phallus that marks the difference between them. Yet, as Judith Butler remarks, they are nonetheless "bound to each other by an essential relation in which that difference is contained." This does not imply that the penis is the privileged referent merely to be displaced or negated, as Butler somewhat problematically asserts (*Bodies That Matter* 90), but is to suggest, perhaps, that the *trace* of the penis remains in the substitutive chain occasioned by the symbolic or discursive instantiation and signification of the phallus.

The mediation of difference between penis and phallus is crucial in any attempt to situate the phallus in relation to fascism, because it is at the juncture of difference—and not metaphor—where the conflation of fascism with homosexuality slips. The fascist desires the visible erection and penetrative power of the phallus (rendered discursively in the bar that maintains all binary oppositions, such as male/female, white/black, active/passive, hetero/homo, and so on), and not necessarily the materiality of the penis itself. Yet, as Hewitt acknowledges, while desire is excited by rigidity, in the end the penis produces only emission and flaccidity—for fascism indicating the collapse of its power not by some external force or opposition, but through the paradoxical interpellation of desiring both totalitarian power (which would include the law of desire) while succumbing to the aggression of fellatio, of being sexually pleasured, and thereby not acquiring the law of desire while having it, indicating a slipping of totalitarian control and a gap in the opposition between control/surrender, active/passive, masculine/feminine. For homosexuals, fellatio would signify differentially. It would not necessarily represent a desire for a rigid phallic order, or for totalitarian power that it might for the fascist, but instead a recognition of the "impossible closure" of desire (Hewitt, "Sleeping with the Enemy" 138), a recognition that no penis is the ultimate phallus, the transcendent object of his desire. On the axis of desire, some degree of intersection between fascism and homosexuality might be able to be arguably theorized, though I would maintain the connection between them remains on shaky ground.[10] However, the attendant spaces of difference, both with respect to the object of desire and its loss for each, point to how the subjects in question are *differentially* articulated and constituted by the signifier, and its difference, its lack, which is the space of desire, and would thereby render the conflation of fascism with homosexuality unstable.

It seems, then, that an attempt to locate fascism as a pathological form of masculine gender identity based on a repudiation of femininity is limiting and relies on homophobic tropes already apparent in heteropatriarchal culture and reinforced, historically speaking, by psychiatric and clinical models of the etiology of homosexuality. What is the political efficacy of resurrecting and recycling such powerful, yet still oppressive discourses (because they still carry cultural weight in explaining homosexuality) and using them against nazi fascists who certainly made use of those very same discourses to justify the persecution of homosexuals and produce propaganda about homosexuality as a public threat? Even if one were to argue that perhaps nazi fascists became so paranoid as to internalize their own propaganda about homosexuality, the tropes of failed or otherwise abject gender (or the fear of that failure or abjection), tied to a feared regression to a more feminine state of non-differentiation as a separate and signifiable self and to the loss of phallic power, still reinscribes homosexuality as a form of pathology, dependent upon the denigration of femininity. This is so even if the object of study has shifted to the fascist as an explanation for the violence exercised and deployed against any perceived threat to masculinity (his own and that of the nation-state) and masculine ego coherence. Moreover, this question is particularly important since propagations of such discourses are by no means restricted to the past, but are differentially redeployed in various strands of contemporary culture, as I shall discuss in the next chapter.

While I have made queer use of psychoanalysis to argue against any simplistic, causal, or symptomatic conflation of homosexuality with fascism, what still remains undeconstructed in psychoanalysis, and in culture more broadly, is femininity in men (either through identification or through its violent, often unconscious, repudiation) as the signifier of homosexuality.[11] As Melanie Hawthorne notes, this not only "rests on the twentieth-century conflation of homosexuality and effeminacy," but relies heavily on ideological ideas about masculinity and femininity (31) within a regime of compulsory heterosexuality that keeps the hierarchies of the genders in place. In psychoanalytic terms, so heavily relied upon as a lens—such as in the work of Theweleit considered earlier in this chapter, which argues that the Freikorpsmen feared reabsorption into a feminine state of undifferentiation and a loss of masculinity—a resistance is enacted as a defense that is fraught with violence against whatever is seen to threaten any loss of stable masculine identity. Though I would argue that the loss might be better understood within a Lacanian framework, and while I would concede, as does Hawthorne, that Theweleit rejects strict Freudian oedipal theory, but relies heavily on psychoanalytic structures to account for the fear of feminine reabsorption (Hawthorne 28), psychoanalytic structures cannot escape the primacy of the oedipal complex so crucial to masculine gender development, since the father is regarded as the source of maternal separation and symbolic acquisition and mastery. If psychoanalysis is to be used as a lens to queer fascism, psychoanalysis simultaneously needs to be queered so as to expose the blind spots in its thinking that maintain cultural hegemonies pertaining to the development of gender and sexuality. Identification with the law of the father is dependent upon a hierarchy of gender and the subordination of women. Moreover, as John Brenkman notes, psychoanalysis has not engaged the pathogenic effects of masculine gender identification at the oedipal phase, and the ways in which the so-called "positive" resolution of the oedipal complex takes its shape from the imperatives of compulsory heterosexuality and is (mis)shaped by the moral dissonance created by misogyny and homophobia that surround it. Moreover, he argues, compulsory heterosexuality, as a regime, offers an imaginary, fantasmatic equivalence between becoming a man and desiring a woman (236–37). Feminist and queer work, in mobilizing around this point, as I've indicated elsewhere, must point to the ruptures in this regime by exposing its gaps, that is, how men who do not identify with hegemonic masculinity may or may not become gay, and how gay men may or may not conform to prescribed gender expectations and may or may not have resisted maternal separation and identification with the father at the oedipal phase, in spite of patriarchal imperatives to do so.[12] Further, since work that accounts for the virility and phallic masculinity of nazi fascists grounds "the adult expressions of fascist tendencies in the pre-oedipal stages of life, in the early childhood issues of separation from the mother and identity formation" (Hawthorne 29–30), the oedipal phase, as a theory of gender identification and formation, is the male child's first separation from femininity, embodying the imperatives of social life, the pathway to the symbolic, and the essentials of culture.

But rather than explaining fascist leanings in psychoanalytic terms uncritically, which can simultaneously denigrate homosexual victims of nazi fascism as pathological, such work needs simultaneously to engage and critique the misogyny and homophobia implicit in psychoanalytic trajectories of gender identification more broadly. Leo Bersani, for instance, has pointed to the traumatic and defensive aspects of the discovery of sexual difference in boys and how they derive the meaning of masculinity through a negating of the image of femininity. This occurs to the extent that the formation of hegemonic, hetero-masculinity in boys depends on a misogynistic identification with the father, and a permanent equating of femininity with castration, which certainly fits the fascist prototype in work that links it to homosexuality. But Bersani suggests that homosexual desire, to the extent that it depends on maternal identification in boys, may have detraumatized sexual difference through internalizing it, thereby setting up a new and different relation with the father not marked as the Law and not based on a flight from femininity (58). The questioning of psychoanalytic tropes pertaining to gender and oedipal identifications—or a rethinking of these, as opposed to simply molding fascist identities to a pre-given psychoanalytic grid of inscription and intelligibility—may help rupture any essential or causal link, that is, any imaginary relation of self-sameness, between fascism and homosexuality.

Further, in order to be more fully attentive to the ways in which it reproduces essentialized genders, work in this area needs to address the undertheorization of women in Holocaust research in general, a point raised and discussed at length in the previous chapter. Scholarship that argues for the root of fascist hypermasculinity and violence as a cover for an underlying femininity only addresses fascist men, masculine gender identity (its achievement or its failure), and male homosexuality, and regards femininity as a disavowed or repressed object while neglecting to address actual women as potential fascist subjects. In the areas of social policy and everyday life, as Brenkman reminds us, feminists continue to expose the private domain of inequality on which the public domain of masculine equality has rested (241). Following from this, if processes of identification and separation/differentiation, understood in oedipal terms, are gendered, and often relegated to the *private* domain—insofar as these psychic processes are psychoanalytically constructed through an understanding of *public* life with social and political effects in the everyday world in terms of how we think about gender—what are the implications of fascist desire for women? Can females experience the same fear of regression to undifferentiation prior to maternal separation, since they have no castration to fear? Can women, asks Hawthorne, be constituted by fascist desire or have access to it, though perhaps not along the same trajectory that has been theorized for men? The problem, similar to research that pays attention to gay male victims of the Third Reich at the expense of lesbians where the axis of gender cannot be ignored, is that the models that describe the formation of fascist subjects rest, according to Hawthorne, upon the problematic assumption that the fascist body is necessarily male, which excludes women from consideration in the first place (32). While women had limited roles in the life of the polis under National Socialism and were often forcefully encouraged, even rewarded for pursuing their roles as wives and mothers (though many women, including lesbians, resisted, as pointed out in the previous chapter), is it possible that the relegation of fascism to the exclusive domain of men might be more of a historical contingency than an inherent trait? The questions that Hawthorne asks are interesting, even if, as she herself concedes, it might be reassuring for women to think of fascism as a pathological problem of phallic masculinity gone awry (32). It might even be more productive from a feminist standpoint not to theorize the possibility of fascist desire in women, but to argue for more feminist-based understandings of democracy and citizenship. But Hawthorne's questions help rupture further not only a conflation of fascism with homosexuality, but a conflation of fascism with masculinity as well, both of which rely on misogynistic and homophobic assumptions that have been left largely unchallenged in the body of work that posits a causal relationship between fascism and male homosexuality.

On the other hand, I am not arguing against any possibility of gay men and women, especially in the interwar years, having fascist leanings or sympathies. As Didier Eribon reminds us, it would be simplistic, given socio-historical conditions at the time, to assume homosexuality as linked exclusively, or even predominately, to left-wing politics, liberal thinking, or socially progressive ideals. This view, argues Eribon, is a relatively recent phenomenon that dates as far back as the 1970s (200) to a post-Stonewall gay politics in the United States. Gay men and lesbians in Europe, in the years leading up to, during, and immediately following World War II, were, according to Eribon, more often than not marked on the right or far right of the political spectrum and were often anti-Semitic (200–201). Locating the source of fascism in homosexuality, and backing this up with a history of homosexual collaboration in France under the nazi occupation,[13] or assuming, on the other hand, that gay men and lesbians have always been associated with more leftist political beliefs and commitments, is contrary to historical realities, and once again reduces the signifier of "homosexuality" (or "gay" or "lesbian") to a singular, univocal meaning, suppressing the multiple ways in which sexual dissidents may be politicized, and how this may vary across and within specific historical contexts. Eribon, in speaking of lesbians and gay men in France in the 1920s and 1930s, notes that many were attracted to fascist ideology because they favored the restoration of a strong, stable (masculinist) social order in the years following World War I that would not disintegrate into the loss of social and economic privilege, which modern social democracies, and especially communism, might—in their view—threaten (192–93).

Attention to social class sheds some light on the fascist attractions of many visible gay men and lesbians in Europe in the 1920s and 1930s, some of whom simply mirrored the values and economic privileges of their social class. Whether aristocratic, or within the social circles of the elite avant-garde artists, writers, and political movements, "le monde gay" of the 1920s of which George A. Chauncey speaks, according to Eribon, was also marked by anti-democratic, and sometimes fascist, leanings (202–3) at a time highly charged with anti-Semitism and a hatred of communism (or the *Front Populaire* in France). Not only does this help point to the multiple ways in which lesbians and gay men are politicized and politically positioned, it also points further to the futility of attempting to align sexual identities with political affiliations while avoiding a sentimentalizing or mythologizing of a queer past. Shari Benstock has written of the problematics in conflating lesbian identities (resistant to the patriarchal imperatives on women's lives centered on marriage and motherhood) with other socially progressive political commitments. Speaking of the artistic avant-garde lesbians in Paris during the interwar years, Benstock notes that while each woman's politics was markedly different, writers such as Gertrude Stein, Natalie Barney (both of whom had artistic salons in Paris that fed off and had an impact on the Modernist movement), Alice B. Toklas, Romaine Brooks, Liane de Pougy, and others shared a sense of privileged and separate social status in Paris (333) that bound them, in different ways, I think, to the era's dominant rightist ideologies, such as fascism.[14] While Paris offered expatriate women such as Barney and Stein the possibility of artistic and sexual freedom in ways Britain or America did not, other aspects of patriarchal thinking nonetheless followed artistic expatriate women to Paris. Benstock writes of Barney's anti-Semitism, her blaming of Jews for both wars so that they could secure greater profits (thereby supporting Pound's anti-Semitic theory of usury), and her overall nazi sympathies. Speaking of Stein, who, unlike Barney, was not a nazi sympathizer, Benstock notes that Stein's anti-Semitism allowed her to turn a blind eye to the fate of fellow Jews and to the gravity of her own situation in nazi-occupied

France. The measures she and Toklas took to safeguard their collection of modern art and Stein's manuscripts in the 1930s were based not on a fear of imminent war against the nazi threat, but on a fear of a communist uprising in France, which would threaten their lifestyle, their economic security through inherited funds, and their political connections in the French government (338–39).

One cannot readily assume that dissident sexualities necessarily created a tear in the fabric of fascism or in any other rightist political ideology that comprised their social worlds. Rather, the extent of resistance to—or complicity with—nazi fascism by lesbians and gay men becomes the question insofar as one may be oppressed by one axis of social positioning (sexuality, gender in the case of lesbians), yet at the same time be enabled by others (race, class). But just as it would be erroneous to reduce fascism to homosexuality, the transhistorical and decontextualized reduction of the politics of lesbians and gay men to radical social reform, a breaking down of class boundaries, or social progressivism would be equally fallacious, given the political commitments of many socially privileged lesbians and gay men during the interwar years to self-protectionism, socio-economic status, and susceptibility to the causes of right-wing ideologies.

The relationship between political allegiance and sexuality is, therefore, one that is fraught with contradiction and difference. Whether one reads the *Freikorps*, or, indeed, high-ranking nazi officials as marked a priori by homo-social bonds, repressed homoeroticism, or latent homosexuality; or all lesbians in the avant-garde culture of Paris in the first part of the twentieth century as reifying, rather than subverting, fascist ideology; one fails to situate the signifier "homosexuality" socially and reduces it to a singular meaning with traces of perversity, while neglecting to ask how it also may have ruptured discursively and politically the totalizing gestures of Third Reich nationalism. Conversely, to read dissident sexualities as inherently in opposition to fascist ideology is equally problematic and reductive without attention to historical context and the insistent pressures of other sites of subjective identification and social affiliation. While attention to the political allegiances of particular individuals under the Third Reich in Germany, or in the occupied territories, may be useful as a step toward a theorization of the various ways in which homosexuality may have signified in relation to nazi power, it is important to examine the multiple meanings of homosexuality as a signifier that circulates in culture—including its gaps and contradictions—in order to avoid the repathologization of homosexuality (through homosexualizing fascism and collaboration) and the mythologization of queer history insofar as one assumes that homosexuality is always already a resistance to dominant forms of power. Not only will attention to the discursive circulation of homosexuality and homophobic strategies of domination allow for more complex queer histories in particular contexts, it will also enable analysis of their continued, yet varied, reinscriptions in culture in the present day.

5

Discursive Traces of Nazi Homophobia in Contemporary Culture

A more explicit theorization of the politics of sexuality under National Socialism helps shed light on distinctive nodes of power and social organization under nazism, including the racialization of sexuality and the specificity of gender difference (which allows for the emergence of a lesbian narrative space and accounts for the ways in which resistant women were also oppressed under nazi rule), and presents challenges to the reductive conflation of nazi fascist hypermasculinity with homosexuality (to the extent that such a conflation reads homosexuality symptomatically and fails to situate it within broader signifying practices). I have thus far argued that nazi homophobia, as it was linked to other forms of power, was by no means a momentary aberration, but was deeply imbricated with particular material, cultural, and historical practices within and prior to the nazi era. In a culture where LGBT (lesbian, gay, bisexual, and transgendered) rights appear to be becoming more intimately enmeshed in western conceptions of human rights, it is nonetheless important to note that material practices still lag behind juridical law, and that the traces of the aberration of nazi homophobia, and their connections to social and historical processes, continue to find expression, though often in less overt ways, in the contemporary social world, especially in consideration of initial responses to the AIDS crisis in the West and in the current global management of HIV/AIDS and its effects in the postcolonial and Third World. Similarly at issue are proliferations of interpretations of homosexuality in postcolonial contexts, where it is becoming increasingly more visible, that proclaim homosexuality as a foreign intrusion in indigenous cultures and therefore an impediment to decolonization. The criminalization of homosexuality in the penal codes of many countries in the world can—and often does—result in harassment, persecution, and punishment, and limits the attainment of full human rights for lesbians, gay men, and other sexual dissidents, even in places where discriminatory laws against gay people exist but are rarely enforced and remain linked nonetheless to state-enforced discrimination against sexual difference. The same is true in the form of "Gender Identity Disorder in Childhood," or GIDC, listed in the current edition of the *Diagnostic and Statistical Manual for Mental Disorders* (or *DSM*), published by the American Psychiatric Association (APA), which is specifically tied to the prevention of gay outcome in gender-atypical children, especially boys. These veiled cultural instantiations of homophobia are condoned by powerful cultural institutions (law, medicine), as was the case under National Socialism, though not necessarily with the same degree of fervor. Yet such instantiations, insofar as they provoke condemnation, discrimination, violence—both psychic and physical—and various forms of social exclusion, real or imagined, against lesbians, gay men, and other sexual dissidents, undermine erotic autonomy and one's basic human rights. But they cannot be understood as reducible to homophobia alone as a separate or isolated vector of domination, but must instead be specifically contextualized in ways I have thus far been arguing, that is, as always already mediated by specific historical, cultural, and ideological conditions.

As I have suggested, the remnants of nazi homophobia did not cease or dissipate with the defeat of nazism at the end of World War II. Just as the National Socialist government built on pre-existing social prejudices surrounding homosexuality prior to its rise to power in 1933 (as I pointed out in chapter 2), the stigmatization and criminalization of homosexuality in the German penal code far outlived the collapse of the Third Reich. In fact, homosexuality remained on the books as a criminal offense (legally punishable by arrest and incarceration) in the German Federal Republic (the former West Germany) until 1969, and homosexuality remained a crime in Austria until 1971. In the German Federal Republic in particular, as Dagmar Herzog notes, continued support for Paragraph 175 after the Third Reich was often based on the protection of German youth from homosexual "seduction" (*Sex after Fascism* 93). Equally important to note, in the aftermath of the war, and for a long time after, is that the German Federal Republic refused to recognize gay men and lesbians as having a status similar to those of other victims persecuted by the nazis. Under the Reparation Act for Those Persecuted under National Socialism, which became law in the Federal Republic of Germany on June 29, 1956, reparation in the amount of fifty million German marks was paid by the mid-1970s as compensation to victims of the nazis incarcerated in camps. Yet as Rüdiger Lautmann notes, the act did not speak to the illegalities of detention, and those in so-called non-political categories (such as gypsies, homosexuals, asocials, criminals, and those persecuted for security reasons) were excluded. In other words, this very narrow definition of the "political" was applied only to conscious and active opposition to the nazis and to those who suffered religious or racial discrimination (356). Shamefully, those who were subjected to nazi persecution and escaped the narrow definition of those who were "politically" prosecuted still experienced the encumbrance of their human rights, and these included homosexuals, who, as Lautmann also notes, were denied claims for compensation even as the category for those entitled to it expanded over time (356–57).[1] The memoir and testimony of one gay survivor of a nazi death camp, who spent six years there and later applied for compensation in Germany but was rejected, is captured in Heinz Heger's *The Men with the Pink Triangle*:

> My request for compensation for the years of concentration camp was rejected by our democratic authorities, for as a pink-triangled prisoner, a homosexual, I had been condemned for a criminal offense, even if I'd not harmed anyone. No restitution is granted to "criminal" concentration-camp victims.... In the early days after my homecoming, the neighbors made a bit of a fuss about this "queer" concentration-camp returnee. But since I led a very quiet life and was never involved in any scandal, they let me go about my work in peace, though none of them went out of their way to be friendly. At first I didn't mind this at all, for I felt no need to talk to other people. Later, however, this rejection became burdensome and depressing. But whether we gays live in Vienna or anywhere else, we can live as decent a life as we want, but the contempt of our fellow humans, and social discrimination, is the same as it was thirty or fifty years ago. The progress of humanity has passed us by. (117)

Because Paragraph 175 of the German penal code criminalized homosexuality, the German government's position in the years immediately after the war was that the sentences passed on to homosexuals under the nazi regime were completely legal. As Günter Grau points out, German politicians in the postwar period believed that the nazi proceedings against homosexuals were legally and socially justified since the nazis acted out of military necessity and within traditional sanctions at the time to prevent criminal behavior. Grau reminds us as well that the Nuremberg trials, which prosecuted former nazis for crimes and atrocities committed against humanity, invoked no crimes committed against homosexuals, nor was there a record of publicized trials in the Federal Republic of Germany or in the German Democratic Republic which called to account prosecutors, judges, military officials, or doctors who took part in the sustained victimization of, and violence toward, those who were homosexual (Grau, "Final Solution of the Homosexual Question?" 339). Not only has this helped to avoid the fuller prosecution of nazi fascist perpetrators, as Grau further indicates (339), but it has enabled the perpetuation of homophobia as a vector of power and domination, while being cloaked in appeals to the law at the time. Most disturbing, as if internment as a homosexual in a concentration camp and the violences inflicted therein by the SS, the *kapo* system, and fellow inmates were not enough, a report of the U.S. Holocaust Memorial Museum indicates that under the Allied Military Government of Germany following the war, some homosexuals were forced to serve out their prison terms regardless of the time spent in concentration camps ("Homosexuals: Victims of the Nazi Era"). Grau notes also that the long-term effects of such socially-entrenched homophobic prejudice, and its ongoing expression that continued after World War II, have generally remained unexplored ("Final Solution" 343). One purpose of this chapter is to initiate such an exploration, not in a linear or empirically historical way, but to expose discursive traces, operating at the nexus of a range of signifying practices and under specific historical and ideological conditions, that are not entirely indistinct, or a world apart, from nazi homophobia, nazi theories of racial purity, and National Socialist fears of social degeneracy.

Well into the postwar period, especially in the United States, homosexuality threatened the social production of stable gender and (hetero)sexual identity. In addition, as Robert J. Corber argues, homosexuals were constructed as national security risks, as those who threatened the system of social representation that characterized Cold War conformity and the consolidation of the Cold War consensus (2–3) in a way similar, though not reducible, to nazi paranoia about social respectability and perceived threats to its national borders. The publication of the Kinsey Report on male sexuality in 1948, which challenged psychiatry's long-held orthodox oppositions between the conflation of normality and abnormality with heterosexuality and homosexuality respectively, questioned seriously the received medical and social wisdom of the time that homosexuality was an aberration and that heterosexuality was the self-evident pinnacle and summation of sexual development and maturity. Along these lines, Kinsey effectively exposed any natural links between heterosexuality and biological reproduction as social constructions that served to maintain heteronormativity. Most important, perhaps, Kinsey found that 37 percent of American males had sexual contact with other men to the point of orgasm and ejaculation between adolescence and old age. There was a range in the men interviewed for their sexual histories that went from those who engaged in no homosexual behavior at all, to those who had engaged in homosexual behavior with varying degrees of frequency, to those who were exclusively homosexual (Kinsey 625, 638). Yet because Kinsey found that homosexuals could be found "in every age group, in every social level, in every conceivable occupation in cities and on farms, and in the most remote areas of the country" (627), his study helped to fuel American nationalist fears that male homosexuals weren't necessarily effeminate and could "pass" as straight. As such, as Corber notes, homosexuals could infiltrate the nation's cultural and political institutions and, like communists, subvert them from within (11).

The fact that gay men could escape detection and easily evade social apparatuses of surveillance and identification was picked up by *Life* magazine in the early 1960s in a special exposé, "Homosexuality in America." While still reifying cultural stereotypes of gay men as favoring professions such as interior decoration, hairstyling, and fashion design; by pointing out that gay men were easily identifiable (in 1964 at least) by their "fluffy" sweaters, tight khaki trousers, and tennis shoes (!) (68); and by representing their masculinity as "obsessive" in leather bars where gay men appeared to be masculine and butch (70), *Life* exposed the general fear felt at the time through its assertion that 85 percent of gay men looked and acted like other (heterosexual, read: normal) men and could not be spotted for certain even by experts (77). The pathologization of homosexuality and its social and medical management were linked in the postwar economic boom to the production and consumption of capital. As Corber argues, the production of new forms of male subjectivity was required for the economic transition to a regime of Fordist production and consumption in the United States after the war (11). Male homosocial bonding experienced in wartime needed to be discouraged, and military psychiatrists assisted in helping to purge known homosexuals from military service in the postwar period, both for those serving at home and abroad.[2] The intensely homophobic climate of the immediate postwar years in America, according to Corber, allowed for no conflict between a returning soldier's masculinity and his subsequent role as breadwinner and homeowner after the war (through submitting passively to the corporate structures where he worked and/or consumed their services), since these roles were centered around the production and consumption of durable goods. Those marked as insufficiently masculine, and therefore under suspicion for possibly being gay (since effeminacy was no longer an obvious marker), were those who refused to settle down and raise a family (11–12). Here the findings of Kinsey were reworked to strategic advantage to mark as insufficiently masculine those who did not conform to the new postwar economic shift, therefore posing a threat to the security of the national imaginary. This is similar, but not reducible, to the ways in which National Socialism defined the boundaries of national belonging (in this case through the production of Aryan children to strengthen the race) by reading homosexuality as a betrayal of, and as a threat to, nationalist ideals and goals.[3]

The means of homosexual exclusion were not only driven economically by postwar restructuring but were also buttressed by psychiatry and psychoanalysis, which, not incoincidentally, developed their most homophobic treatises on homosexuality in the 1950s and early 1960s. In 1952, Irving Bieber and his colleagues at the New York Society of Medical Psychoanalysts, in response to the Kinsey Report, growing public awareness of homosexuality, and the anxieties about the difficulty of its detection, began a ten-year investigation of the etiology of homosexuality. Their research was published in the 1962 book *Homosexuality: A Psychoanalytic Study of Male Homosexuals* and, for a time, was the standard pronouncement on male homosexuality for the psychiatric community and the general public.[4] In the study, Bieber found "effeminacy" in the childhoods of the 106 gay male patients studied (the H group) to be a significant distinguishing factor as compared to the 100 heterosexual men in the control group (the C group in the study). Childhood effeminacy, as reported by the patient in analysis and then submitted by the patient's analyst to the researcher,[5] found patterns of "prehomosexual childhood" in the men of the H group, such as excessive fear of physical injury in 75 percent, girls as primary playmates in a third, and participation in the usual games and pastimes of boys in less than one-fifth (Bieber et al. 204). Further, 25 percent of patients in the H group exhibited such physical behaviors as exaggerated shrugging, "wrist-breaking," lisping, hand-to-hip posturing, and effusiveness (188–89). Most disturbing, the Bieber team chose to reject Freud's theorization of the role of constitutional factors in the development of homosexuality and shifted attention instead to oedipal and pre-oedipal experiences and familial relationships.[6] This resulted in the promulgation of the by-now-all-too-familiar trope of "close-binding" mothers who stimulated their sons through over-close intimacy and seductiveness, thwarted the development of heterosexual drives, and interfered with their sons' relationships to their fathers and with peers, both of whom would enable maternal separation (Bieber et al. 79–81). As I have pointed out elsewhere, this is a particular point at which homophobia and misogyny intersect in culture,[7] as it did similarly under National Socialism to the extent that homosexuality was associated with femininity and feminine identifications, and therefore with weakness.

In the same year that the Bieber study began, the American Psychiatric Association (APA) published its first official listing of mental disorders in the form of the *Diagnostic and Statistical Manual of Mental Disorders*, more commonly known as the *DSM*. The first edition of the *DSM*, known subsequently as *DSM-I* following the publication of several revised editions, was an attempt by American psychiatry, as Ronald Bayer argues, to establish the boundaries of its work (39), and the first edition listed homosexuality as a sociopathic personality disturbance. Similarly, as has been discussed earlier, the nazis viewed homosexuality in pathological and sociopathic terms, especially in relation to their population policies. By the mid-1930s, according to Robert B. Proctor, medical literature in Germany documented the supposedly pathological character of male homosexuality, and physicians in particular were arguing that homosexuality, medically speaking, posed a threat to public health (212). But more interesting, while many nazi doctors believed homosexuality to be genetic and biologically determined, unlike their postwar psychiatric counterparts, there were many medical positions in nazi Germany that disputed this claim by arguing that the view of homosexuality as inherited simply played into the ideology of homosexual politics to the extent that homosexuals simply could claim that they were unable to change their sexual behavior. One nazi doctor argued that homosexual men were like Jews because homosexuals were "not 'poor, sick' people to be treated, but enemies of the state to be eliminated" (qtd. in Proctor 213). There seems to be a tendency on the part of both the Bieber study and some nazi doctors to situate homosexuality socially as a conscious or learned rebellion against prevailing social and cultural norms, which rendered homosexuals enemies of the state under nazism, and later rendered them in the Cold War era as more culturally (i.e., medically) legible as the result of early pathological family dynamics. In both cases, homosexuality could be "treatable" through "re-education" under the nazis for "opportunistic" homosexuals, and treatable through the self-serving rubric of counseling and "treatment" for more "healthy" parent-child relations (for families) and psychiatric evaluation and care (for homosexuals) in postwar psychiatric and medical contexts.

The Bieber study eventually lost its authoritarian status on the subject of homosexuality and its grasp on dominant clinical thinking by the late 1960s, largely because of its predisposition to pathology and by studying only gay men as a clinical population, and because of the rise and influence of social activism and debates within the psychiatric and medical communities about the diagnostic status of homosexuality. While homosexuality was eventually deleted as a diagnostic category from the *DSM* in a historic 1973 decision by the APA and did not appear in the next edition of the *DSM* (*DSM-III*, published in 1980),[8] Bieber's blatantly homophobic and misogynistic interpretation of homosexuality has made an indelible mark on more recent clinical work on "Gender Identity Disorder in Childhood" (or GIDC), which, not incoincidentally, entered the *DSM-III* as a new category of diagnosis. That is, GIDC appeared in the same edition of the *DSM* from which homosexuality was first deleted.[9] The current issue of the *DSM* (*DSM-IV*) still contains an entry for "Gender Identity Disorder in Childhood" and indicates that boys are more commonly referred for treatment for GIDC at a ratio of about five to one (*DSM-IV* 535); the gender difference in terms of the therapeutic imposition of a diagnosis of GIDC on gender-atypical boys, as I have argued elsewhere, is a social and cultural phenomenon that psychiatry and psychoanalysis, as clinical *and* cultural practices, have yet to address and explain (Spurlin, "Sissies and Sisters" 82). In boys, the *DSM* says that their gender "disorder" is often manifested by a preoccupation with traditionally feminine activities, including cross dressing, preferences for the stereotypical games and pastimes of girls, including playing with "female-type" dolls, drawing pictures of beautiful princesses, identifying with female heroines in books or on television, and taking the role of the mother in playing house, while usually avoiding "rough-and-tumble" play (533). These behaviors are not remarkably different from the "prehomosexual childhoods" of the homosexual patients Bieber studied in the 1950s.

The same trend of pathologizing gender atypicality in children continues among more contemporary clinicians who work on GIDC. Richard C. Friedman, for example, who was on the Advisory Committee on Psychosexual Disorders for the *DSM-III* and applauds the decision of the APA to drop homosexuality from the *DSM*, wrote as late as 1988 that when "homosexual phenomena" are symptomatic of primary psychiatric disorder, such as gender identity disorder, they should be so specified in the manual (186). While Friedman attempts to distance himself from the earlier pathological model, which nonetheless serves as his intertext, he still relies on certain types of family dynamics that lead to gender atypicality and homosexual possibility. This is seen clearly in his assertion that families of gender-atypical boys are marked by active maternal involvement discouraging separation and individuation and by the absence or detachment of the father. Moreover, Friedman asserts quite rigidly that boys develop their gender identity in the context of separating from the mother and that psychological movement away from maternal intimacy (which threatens male gender identity) stems from the necessity to create distance from the mother (238). Other researchers, such as Kenneth Zucker and Susan Bradley, internationally known experts on GIDC, affirm as late as 1995 that gender identity disorder in boys "arises out of the interaction between a boy's temperamental vulnerability to high arousal and an insecure mother-child relationship" (262).

While the earlier pathological model of homosexuality proffered by Bieber et al., as well as work by Sandor Rado, Edmund Bergler, Charles Socarides, and others,[10] interpreted male homosexuality as sociopathic and then as psychopathological—as manifested in gender-atypical behavior and the failure of maternal separation in boys—"revisionary" work on GIDC seems more accepting of homosexuality in adult men as a sex-gender object choice that cannot be changed. This work is driven instead by the prevention of homosexual outcome and by the social anxieties and phobias raised by the specter of feminine boys. Yet whose interests are served in pathologizing and treating nonconformity to culturally prescribed gender roles as a "disorder"? Here there is not only the conflation of gender with sexuality (that is, gender typicality = heterosexuality), which admittedly made the social detection of homosexuals difficult for the nazis and during the later Cold War atmosphere of paranoia, since it was soon realized in both contexts and periods that not all homosexual men were gender atypical. But there is also the more culturally problematic conflation of psychological health with social conformity, which, as Bayer notes, enables the category of "health" (psychological or otherwise) to become a moral category to ideologically justify discriminatory social practices (13). It was this more abhorrent conflation that was taken up by the nazis to mark homosexuals as social outsiders, degenerates, and enemies of the state as discussed in chapter 2.

Yet the conflation of psychological health with social conformity was not entirely absent in postwar psychiatric work on the etiology of homosexuality, nor has it been absent in more contemporary clinical work on GIDC. It is the discursive and material strategies of exclusion that must be identified, rather than only specific instances of homophobia as a single vector of domination alone, in order to appreciate fully the continuities of nazi homophobia since the time of the Third Reich and the seedlings of their ramifications in wider systemic exclusionary practices in the postwar period and in the present day. The prevention of homosexuality and the linking of psychological health with social conformity informed the clinical work of Bieber et al., as well as more recent work on GIDC. Eve Sedgwick has spoken of the ongoing and continuing lack of institutionalized resistance to the wish endemic in culture that gay people not exist, which is not a far cry from the systematic exclusion of homosexuals, supported through an array of social institutions, under the Third Reich:

> The scope of institutions whose programmatic undertaking is to prevent the development of gay people is unimaginably large. There is no major institutionalized discourse that offers a firm resistance to that undertaking; in the United States, at any rate, most sites of the state, the military, education, law, penal institutions, the church, medicine, and mass culture enforce it all but unquestioningly, and with little hesitation at even the recourse to invasive violence. ("How To Bring Your Kids Up Gay" 161)

While GIDC seems to meet the needs of anxious parents who may fear they have a gay child, the issue seems to be more of a critical questioning of their motives for actively, or subtlely, discouraging gender-atypical identifications and behaviors in their children, especially boys, and reflecting not merely on the possibility, but on the utter *desirability*, of parenting a queer child. This could be a necessary first step in the depathologization of the gender-atypical child in particular, and of homosexuality more broadly, which still retains the remnants of pathology despite its removal from the *DSM* thirty-five years ago.

More contemporary traces of the socially systemic stigmatization of homosexuality in relation to other axes of power, however, are no more apparent than in official responses to HIV/AIDS (government, local/global health policies, and immigration laws to name a few) early in the pandemic in western countries, particularly in the United States, and in ongoing responses in much of the developing and postcolonial world. Less than a mere ten years after the American Psychiatric Association's 1973 decision to delete homosexuality as a category of diagnosis in the *DSM*, the onset and recognition of HIV/AIDS as a medical condition in the early 1980s (before the isolation of the human immunodeficiency virus) brought about the emergence of new discourses of sexual perversion centered on metaphors of social defiance, erotic indulgence, hedonism, and moral laxity through the transmission of HIV either sexually or through shared needles used intravenously. Those who were ill, and, as Susan Sontag points out, those diagnosed with HIV seropositivity, were cast as deserving of blame (*AIDS and Its Metaphors* 26) because most of the victims at the time seemed to be "disposable" groups insofar as gay men and intravenous drug users were identified as the major risk groups for acquiring the virus that brought about AIDS and AIDS-related conditions. In the United States, those early assumptions of HIV/AIDS resulted in government inaction and a highly indifferent medical establishment until HIV began to spread into the dominant population. Further, as Cindy Patton, one of the most distinguished social and cultural critics on the subject of AIDS, observes, the simultaneous emergence of HIV and President Ronald Reagan's overall plan to shift the role of government services to communities (under the guise of Christian charity and volunteerism) ignored the overall systemic disenfranchisement not only of homosexuals but of racial and ethnic minorities as well through proposed strategies of defunding (Patton, *Inventing AIDS* 16; 140n). It is important to note that in the period prior to the initial classification of Acquired Immune Deficiency Syndrome, and in the immediate period thereafter, the emergence of AIDS heightened homophobia because of its association with gay men and accompanying stereotypes of promiscuity in the early to mid-1980s. Yet, as Patton notes, little attention was paid to the failure of Reagan funding for drug and poverty programs at a time when

AIDS was exacerbating these longstanding problems (*Inventing AIDS* 16–17). In this regard, then, the homophobia surrounding HIV/AIDS cannot be separated from a broader range of social and political contextualizations surrounding race and class, a point to which I shall return in a moment.

My purpose here is not to write a social or cultural history of AIDS and activist responses to it, as this has been documented elsewhere. What I wish to point to is the inaction and ignorance of western governments, particularly in the United States, when gay men were falling ill to what was then considered to be an unnamable syndrome or "gay disease." Patton refers to this period as that prior to the Name of AIDS (*Globalizing AIDS* 4), which lasted until the U.S. Center for Disease Control (CDC) defined AIDS as Acquired Immune Deficiency Syndrome in September 1982.[11] Even until the time that the HIV virus was isolated and a blood test developed to detect antibodies in response to the presence of HIV in the blood, HIV/AIDS was still thought to be confined largely to gay men and intravenous drug users, and there was little understanding about the epidemiology of HIV/AIDS outside of these communities. Such thinking by the Reagan administration, the medical profession, and the media helped to create a huge vacuum in the development of prevention programs, since there was no notion, as Patton argues, that recreational drug injection could be occurring in the "safe" suburbs and not only in the inner cities, and that men who did not necessarily identify as gay could be having sex with other men (*Inventing AIDS* 36). At the same time, the Moral Majority in the United States, led by Pat Robertson and the late Jerry Falwell, offered diagnoses of AIDS as divine punishment on a society gone awry. This pronouncement was particularly aimed at homosexuality in the Reagan era, and while it not only perpetuated stereotypes and misunderstandings of the threat of HIV/AIDS, it also affected governmental decisions about funding for research, prevention, and treatment programs.

Once activists began responding to government and medical inaction and challenging the scientific veneer of objectivity and political neutrality pertaining to the discourses and rhetorical strategies through which scientific knowledge made AIDS culturally legible, the Helms Amendment of 1988 restricted language and concepts that could be used in any AIDS education program funded by the U.S. government, thus putting these programs at risk if they were thought to be too "pro-sex" (Patton, *Globalizing AIDS* 13). The consequences of the amendment created a further lag in the development of meaningful safer-sex campaigns and organizing beyond the advocacy of complete sexual abstinence. A politics came into being that simply was not possible under National Socialism, to the extent that social activists in the United States began to challenge not only the idea that societal homophobia is a single vector of domination, unaffected by race and class, but also challenged seriously the discursive and rhetorical representation of AIDS in the public sphere and the simultaneous policing of bodies inhabited by HIV/AIDS.

I point this out because the gap created not only the delay of prevention programs for communities initially at risk for HIV infection (and later for the general population), but because early sufferers of AIDS were largely marked as invisible by a disease syndrome that initially had no name. This was a form of silenced trauma whereby the specificity of the harm was not yet fully named in the early 1980s and was kept out of public view. According to Patton, the pandemic gained its social meaning by building on already deeply-seated prejudices surrounding race, class, gender, sexuality, addiction, and those who suffered the ravages of illness and the specter of decadence and decay associated with this yet-unnamed and little-understood syndrome we soon learned to call AIDS. That is, those who had HIV were seen initially as isolated cases, and this helped to erase the social realities that shaped the growing pandemic (*Inventing AIDS* 25). The period prior to the official naming of AIDS links to Lyotard's *differend*, as Patton mentions, whereby one not only suffers harm—such as having a disease or a condition which is not yet named and simply associated with the abject—but one is simultaneously deprived of the means to express that harm (*Globalizing AIDS* 5). More precisely, the Lyotardian *differend* is the not yet named or the not yet spoken; it is, according to Lyotard, "the unstable state and instant of language wherein something which must be able to be put into phrases cannot yet be" (Lyotard 13). Indeed, the lack of a name for the suffering caused by what we now know as AIDS made it especially difficult for earlier sufferers with HIV/AIDS because they could not name their trauma as there was simply no term for it. Further, the *differend* does not only imply the early lack of a referent in language for HIV infection and AIDS, but the ongoing contingencies surrounding HIV/AIDS (who is at risk, who will fall ill, who will die?), and the perpetual gap and still unnameable space between who is infected with HIV and *who* has the right to be heard and receive care. This gap has been exacerbated by a history of neglect and indifference in the early years of the pandemic by government officials, the medical profession, and the media, who defined "good health" through such vectors as whiteness, western location, middle-class values, hard work, productivity, moderate habits, rationality, and emotional self-control as safeguards against the licentiousness, sexual indulgences, and addictive behaviors that would lead to decadence and disease.

With new drug therapies such as AZT and ddI becoming available by the end of the 1980s that could slow progression of AIDS-related illnesses in HIV-positive people with no symptoms of such illnesses, a marked medical and cultural shift occurred in the history of HIV/AIDS: it became a treatable rather than necessarily a fatal condition. In the 1990s, other new therapies, such as protease inhibitors in 1995, and the viral load test, which provided information on the risk of disease progression, were developed as ways to delay the disease's progress and prolong life. Activism that exposed government and medical complacency and indifference early in the pandemic culminated in the ACT UP (AIDS Coalition to Unleash Power) slogan in 1987, Silence = Death, an appeal, perhaps, to the therapeutic property of discourse, which, according to Lee Edelman, invokes the rhetoric and form of mathematical or scientific inevitability (A = B). The slogan was positioned against the inverted pink triangle (pointed at the top this time) reminiscent of the nazi pogrom against homosexuals in order to appeal to the equivalent of the post-Holocaust discursive position of "Never again" ("The Plague of Discourse" 292). But as Edelman further implies, discourses on AIDS are so volatile and occupy such contentious spaces in the public sphere that they can serve the purposes of social activism to promote understanding of HIV/AIDS and its various victims, including gay men, and simultaneously be marshaled into the service of a contradictory logic of homophobia ("The Plague of Discourse" 303–4).[12] Such therapeutic approaches, whether chemical or discursive, and while somewhat significant in curtailing the progression of HIV/AIDS through treatment with drug therapies and through education and prevention programs in *particular* individuals in *particular* parts of the world, produce neither bodies immune from disease, nor social discourses immune from prejudice and ignorance about AIDS, but simultaneously invoke the Lyotardian *differend* exponentially in other directions.

One such direction, in spite of new drug therapies, such as the protease inhibitors developed in the mid-1990s and a heightened degree of AIDS activism and AIDS education in the United States under the Clinton administration, occurs at the nexus of HIV/AIDS, race, and class, as similarly located in Ronald Reagan's defunding of drug, poverty, and other social programs under the so-called New Altruism mentioned earlier. The same nexus of HIV/AIDS, race, and class operates and is reformulated in a 1996 cover story for *The New York Times Magazine* entitled "When Plagues End: Notes on the Twilight of an Epidemic." In the story, Andrew Sullivan, also the author of the 1995 book *Virtually Normal: An Argument about Homosexuality*, views protease inhibitors optimistically, that is, as a possible end to the plague of AIDS, given that these relatively new therapies were seen as having the potential to reduce the level of HIV in the blood of an infected person to undetectable levels.[13] Sullivan writes that "the vast majority of HIV-positive people in the world, and a significant minority in America, will not have access to the expensive and effective new drug treatments now available. And many Americans—especially blacks and Latinos—will still die" (54). While Sullivan claims, rather unconvincingly, to understand the fact that so many victims of AIDS will die despite the new drug therapies he cites, he argues that HIV infection "no longer signifies death. It merely signifies illness" (54).

But illness instead of death for whom? Sullivan seems very un-self-reflexive in terms of his own position as a white, British-born, middle-class, gay male living in the United States, his relative privilege, and that of his cohort for whom he claims a profound change in the nature of a diagnosis of HIV infection. Sullivan's declaration assumes not only a disavowal of death, but, as Phillip Brian Harper argues, a worrying disavowal of the *significance* of the deaths of those not included in the normative national, racial, and class boundaries Sullivan sets up in defining the impact of protease inhibitors on HIV/AIDS (Harper 8). Here, not entirely indistinct from discourses on homosexuality in the public sphere under National Socialism, homosexuality is (re)racialized, this time under tropes of normative whiteness (read: gay, male, middle class, western), with racial and class hierarchies invoked and sustained with regard to those who might benefit most from new drug therapies to combat HIV/AIDS. The plight of racial and ethnic minorities, as well as indigenous people in the Third World, who may also be infected with the virus, are reduced to a mere passing reference. Moreover, Sullivan's interpellation by *The New York Times*, what Harper refers to as Sullivan's official designation as the "properly public homosexual subject," carries the weight of serious professional journalism and gives Sullivan the power to "rule out of consideration the life experiences of individuals whom he has condemned in their nonnormativity" (Harper 13).

It would be erroneous, indeed obviously dangerous, in the present pandemic, to reduce dissident sexualities straightforwardly to liberal-progressive politics without attention to other sites of subjective identification and social affiliation. As I mentioned in the previous chapter, many socially visible gay men and lesbians during the interwar years in Europe mirrored, to a large extent, the social values and economic privilege of their social class. They either supported, or were not particularly opposed to, fascism, which brings to mind the often fractured and contradictory relations between political allegiance and sexual dissidence, and can shed light on and expose vast differences and inequities in more current discourses on HIV/AIDS among those already publicly marked as gay, and victimized, in varying ways, by HIV/AIDS as a social group.

Sexuality is further racialized through discourses on HIV/AIDS in the global sphere in terms of its configuration in the developing world, especially in Africa.

It was initially assumed that AIDS originated on the so-called dark continent and subsequently spread to Haiti, the United States and Canada, and Europe as a sort of tropical disease or infestation from the Third World. AIDS was also initially regarded as what Susan Sontag has referred to as "a scourge of the *tristes tropiques*," and this was buttressed by racist stereotypes surrounding black and indigenous African sexuality that conflated it with animality and licentiousness (*AIDS and Its Metaphors* 51–52). Such readings, of course, are effects of a legacy of imperialism and colonial control, whereby Africa, according to Emmanuel Eze, has been read paradigmatically as the "mythical" world against which the West can establish itself, in contrast, as representative of a modern, "rational" worldview (49–50). Such a view, which in spite of western imperial domination of Africa, transatlantic slavery, and ideologies of white racial supremacy dating from at least the seventeenth century, still reads Europe as scientific, socially differentiated, and familiar, and Africa as animistic, socially totalistic, and alien (Eze 58).

But with the reliance of the World Health Organization (WHO) on the rhetorical strategies and medical thoughtstyles of tropical medicine, which aims to protect the white European body from "foreign" infections, and epidemiology, which shifts the emphasis of the study of HIV/AIDS from its specific location to its temporal and statistical distribution, both of which inform global representations and policies on AIDS, Patton has exposed how these two medical thoughtstyles are by no means scientifically objective or politically neutral but layered with social ideologies through their power "to structure the terms through which bodies become visible as the locations of disease" (*Globalizing AIDS* 26). This connection of the clinical or scientific domain to the political, that is, to the ideologies and practices of the state, is quite similar to the medical construction of homosexuality under National Socialism as well as to earlier work on the etiology of homosexuality during the Cold War and subsequent revisionary work on homosexuality under the guise of GIDC more recently. While the main mode of transmission of HIV in the West was thought to be through unprotected anal intercourse between men (Pattern One), this helped to construct further racist readings of Africa as sexually decadent, given the significant number of AIDS cases in the 1980s among black immigrants in Europe and North America. Sexuality amongst indigenous Africans was considered to be sexually decadent not in terms of the sex-gender object choice (as it was for homosexuals in the West), but in the *forms* of sexual acts, since it was assumed initially that the primary mode of HIV transmission in Africa was through heterosexual intercourse (Pattern Two). As a result, and somewhat similar to Andrew Sullivan's invocation of social normativities pertaining to race and class in discussing promising treatments for gay men infected with HIV in the West, North Americans in particular, as Patton points out, became quickly convinced that because AIDS in Africa was different in terms of its transmission routes and whom it infected, "ordinary people" (i.e., straight, native-born, white, middle class) could not contract HIV during "ordinary" heterosexual intercourse (*Globalizing AIDS* xiii–xiv). The racialization of sexuality in both cases is stitched together and sustained by the deliberate othering of those placed on the outside of social normativities by race and class, and not necessarily by sexuality alone. This is similar to the ways in which nazi racializations of sexuality were informed by racial hierarchies based on ideologies of Aryan superiority.

Racialized readings of African sexuality, pathologized through the form(s) of heterosexual relations, has not only been inscribed in the global management of AIDS since the early days of the pandemic, but is perpetuated and continued in the present day. For instance, an article on AIDS in southern Africa in a 2002 issue of *The Economist* begins with a rather voyeuristic narrative of some sexual practices in Botswana, describing how some indigenous men prefer what is known as "dry sex." This is a practice whereby indigenous African women, in order to provide more pleasure to their male partners, insert toothpaste or herbs into their vaginas to inhibit the natural secretions that lubricate the vaginal opening. The practice, however, can lead to tears in the vaginal tissue and to bleeding during penetration, which can, in turn, allow the human immunodeficiency virus to more easily penetrate the tissue and enter the bloodstream ("Fighting Back" 27). While the practice could place the woman at risk for infection—provided the male partner is HIV-infected—beginning an article about HIV/AIDS in southern Africa with "dry sex" textually (re)produces an orientalist erotics that imagines non-western exotic otherness as a site of sexual excess, supposedly far removed from the sexual epistemologies and practices of the West.

More specifically, earlier assumptions that HIV in Africa was primarily transmitted through heterosexual intercourse not only elided completely the sexual practices of those indigenous men who had sex with other men, including anal intercourse, but also created a gap and delay in education and prevention programs targeted for that specific group. South Africa, in particular, has the highest HIV-positive population worldwide, presently estimated to be about 5.7 million of its total population of over 47 million. In 2004, the South African government began to provide anti-retroviral drugs to those South Africans who were HIV positive and could not afford them, starting in Gauteng, South Africa's richest province, with distribution in other provinces following.[14] But it is estimated that the drugs are reaching only a small percentage of the people who need them. In fact, the distribution of anti-retroviral medication has been so slow that, according to a report of the World Health Organization, only 33 percent of South Africans in need of treatment have been reached as of the end of 2006 (WHO, "Towards Universal Access"). It remains unclear, then, if the demand for treatment will be able to match resources. And it is unclear if a diagnosis of HIV will signify a manageable disease, as is often assumed to be the case in the West (though this is loaded with racial and class biases), as opposed to the eventual death sentence it has signified in South Africa and in other parts of Africa for so long.

The delay in treatment can be traced to highly racialized readings of African sexuality coming from both the West and from African cultural nationalism. As I pointed out in my book *Imperialism within the Margins*, initial rationales articulated by western-based pharmaceutical companies for not making anti-retroviral drugs more widely available at affordable prices for the five to six million HIV/AIDS sufferers in South Africa asserted or implied that many poor indigenous Africans, who lacked watches and basic literacy skills, would not be able to adhere to the strict regimen required to take prescribed medications at specified times. Missed dosages, or so reasoned the pharmaceutical companies at the time (as reported by the London *Observer* in 2003), could risk the possibility of the emergence of a new drug-resistant strain of HIV ("Aids Orphans' Survival" 5; cited in Spurlin, *Imperialism within the Margins* 119). In addition to globally articulated myths that poor, indigenous Africans somehow cannot be trusted with sophisticated drugs to fight AIDS-related illnesses, South African President Thabo Mbeki's failure to provide effective leadership on AIDS for his country, and his earlier controversial denials of the efficacy of anti-retroviral drugs because of their high price and toxicity, have unwittingly invoked and buttressed racist ideologies, as Cindy Patton points out, that see African countries as too poor to be saved (*Globalizing AIDS* 131).[15] What is the alternative—simply to allow poor indigenous Africans to die as a result of the deliberate unevenness of access to capital (and thereby to treatment and care) and the lack of the means to better economic development and self-sufficiency in sub-Saharan Africa in general by a western, capitalist system that inscribes Africa, discursively and economically, as "a continent apart"? Is this not the beginning of a form of covert or subtle genocide, of the marking of particular racial groups as "disposable," even though complete and systematic annihilation may not be the explicit or intended goal? Where does one draw the line? If we have learned anything at all from the Holocaust and from the atrocities of nazi rule, it must be recalled that it is precisely this kind of dehumanization that allowed genocidal thinking before and during the nazi rise to power to develop and occur.

The racialization of sexuality, however, is not only confined to white, western readings of black sexuality, but has also occurred in African cultural nationalism in the name of postcolonial resistance to the historical precedent of colonial rule. Under the rubric of shaking off the last vestiges of imperial influence in indigenous African cultures, homosexuality is often cast aside in the national imaginaries of many African countries (and in many postcolonial nations elsewhere) as a white, western aberration that is inherently alien to indigenous cultures. While imperial rule certainly regulated sexuality through the policing of rigidly prescribed gender roles within the historically and culturally-specific spaces of the colonies (since this helped to justify its "civilizing mission"), African cultural nationalist discourses in particular, since independence, project a mirror image of imperial constructions of unbridled African sexuality to the extent that indigenous lesbians and gay men are cast as supporting "lifestyles that are no more than invidious imports of empire" (McClintock 384), thereby reflecting a contamination of African cultural purity. Yet the postcolonial nation-state's fantasy of itself as masculine, and then feminized by the imperial imprint of homosexuality, and its appeals to a mythological past that attempt to reify an inherited precolonial heterosexuality, make use of and reinvent similar tropes of abject gender and rearticulate a homophobic discursive grid quite similar to the white imperialist legacies that have had their basis in the West, and which such nationalist claims otherwise purport to resist.[16]

Yet it must be pointed out that the idea of homosexuality being a foreign, western intrusion into indigenous postcolonial cultures in Africa has its roots in a history of imperialism tied to deep-seated historical anxieties about western discursive appropriations of African sexuality in decadent terms. These appropriations, and the anxieties of African cultural nationalism that surround them, remain in discourses surrounding the global surveillance and tracking of HIV infection. The effect of the bifurcation of imperialist and racist readings of African sexuality, and the reluctance of African nations to admit to a presence of homosexuality within their borders, resulted initially in the denial of the practice of anal intercourse among indigenous African men who have sex with other men. This created a significant gap and subsequent delay in education and prevention programs, not to mention treatment options, among groups of men who escaped the gender/sexual categories of the West, given that WHO saw HIV transmission in Africa initially in heterosexual terms, and given that when WHO focused on same-sex transmission between men in Africa, it failed to recognize that some men practiced anal sex with other men while not necessarily identifying as gay. A form of discursive colonization was thus instantiated early in the pandemic among HIV educators working in Africa under the World Health Organization's Global Programme on AIDS (GPA) to the extent that western interpretations of homosexuality, and the imposition of such interpretations on indigenous African men who had sex with men, assumed not only a conflation of anal sex with homosexuality (which would be a problematic conflation for gay sexual practices in the West as well), but the more problematic conflation of sexual *practice* with sexual *identity*. Once HIV educators realized that heterosexual intercourse was not the only mode of HIV transmission in Africa and began to realize that men who had sex with men were also at risk, they initially failed to take into account the fact that indigenous men could have sex with other men and not take on a gay identity as it is understood in the West, since they could take on a "safe" identity that would be more legibly heterosexual. While the spread of HIV/AIDS has reached such high proportions in South Africa and other parts of Africa, no genitally penetrative form of sexual relations is particularly safe, and those who formulated prevention programs brought their own western assumptions of homosexuality to Africa and therefore missed a significant group of men who could have been at risk for transmission and/or infection with the human immunodeficiency virus. Had this been taken into account, it would have had the effect of ascertaining more accurate rates of HIV infection and developing more timely safer-sex campaigns and access to drugs, treatment, and care. Yet this did not occur to the extent that GPA workers failed initially to take into account the more fluid shifts, the more contested borders, between hetero- and homosexuality within indigenous contexts.

Despite the catastrophic effects of the AIDS pandemic in Africa and the delayed responses to it locally and globally in much of the postcolonial world, the interaction of local activists and global interventions though the World Health Organization and the United Nations in AIDS education and AIDS prevention programs and treatment plans has helped, on some level, to decolonize desire. Yet the stigmatization of disease associated with the effects of HIV seropositivity, and the specter of suffering from the effects of AIDS-related illnesses, are still rampant and even legally endorsed in other parts of the world. For instance, according to Amnesty International's recent report on crimes of hate, torture, and ill treatment of gay men, lesbians, and other sexual dissidents, some Caribbean governments, such as those of Trinidad and Tobago, defend sodomy laws and the criminalization of homosexuality in the name of AIDS prevention and the defense of local cultural values. Yet such laws remain oblivious to their effects insofar as they breed and justify violence against gay people (Amnesty International 15; hereafter cited as AI). Furthermore, the association of HIV/AIDS with homosexuality, and the conflation encoded into juridical law, is not only reductive and discriminatory, but it can, as the UN Human Rights Committee has argued, operate effectively as an obstacle to work in HIV prevention (AI 17).

While activism in the West and in other parts of the world has helped to thwart the deployment of homophobia and racialized notions of sexuality in ways not possible (at least overtly) under National Socialism, this should not blind us to the ongoing and debilitating effects of homophobia, racism, and class biases in terms of those who suffer with HIV/AIDS within particular ethnic and racial groups in the West, those living with AIDS in postcolonial countries to the extent that they are seen as betraying their own national or cultural values (homosexuality and AIDS as un-African or un-Islamic), and the poor living and dying with AIDS all over the globe. In many parts of the world, including the West, not only is gender atypicality read as the visible signifier of homosexuality, and therefore of pathology, but the same is often true of HIV/AIDS, which seals homosexuality's pathological status in contrast to the so-called general population, always read as heterosexual and—in the initial phases of the pandemic (though the legacy still persists)—as innocent.

Populations hardest hit by HIV/AIDS often cannot compete linguistically with the more powerful discourses that oppress and silence them. Lyotard reminds us, as I mentioned earlier, that human beings who had assumed they could use language as an instrument of communication learn, through the feeling of pain that accompanies silence, that they are summoned to language, not to make use of existing idioms to name their lived experience of suffering, but to recognize instead that what remains to be said far exceeds that which presently can be phrased (13). Language must be accounted for as always already ideologically loaded and as shaping particular worldviews rather than only being the means by which one consciously attempts to name one's world. Seeing language as much as a symbolic system *and* as a social invention situates it politically; thus Lyotard's theory of the *differend*, in conjunction with the discursive traces of various forms of oppression of lesbians and gay men since National Socialism that I have been discussing in this chapter, reminds us that language can be used as a political tool, and as a form of oppression, insofar as existing idioms are the inventions of dominant social groups to mark the other as such. Discursive and rhetorical strategies and idioms of othering were used under National Socialism in the appropriations of lesbians, gay men, Jews, Roma, Sinti, and other groups the nazis considered to be enemies of the state, as they were similarly present in the powerful medical and psychiatric discourses on homosexuality in the postwar period and in ongoing work on Gender Identity Disorder in Childhood, or GIDC, since the *DSM-III*.

While the discursive practices in the case of medical interpretations of homosexuality and GIDC are not entirely reducible to the ways in which the nazis marked Jews and other groups as social outsiders, the power of such discourses over subordinate social groups to name and appropriate them as such is familiar. There is also a marked similarity to powerful discourses of postcolonial nationalisms that view homosexuality among indigenous men and women as a betrayal of nation and cultural heritage, as there is in the case of medical discourses on AIDS (early in the pandemic and now more globally) in terms of the ways in which AIDS sufferers have been marked by sexual deviance, moral laxity, and licentiousness, and the ways in which such markings are shaped by culturally stereotypical assumptions pertaining to race, class, and geopolitical spatialization. Such inflammatory rhetoric coming from persons in positions of power has enticed—and even encouraged—continued violence against sexual dissidents, as it is often seen to be condoned officially, and often occurs, as it did under the nazis, without impunity, without restitution for victims, and without official reparation.

Another site of contemporary homophobia lies with those often most unable to resist it worldwide: women and children. In the case of gay and lesbian youth, the official voices of heteronormative power are even more influential, not only in terms of children referred for treatment for a clinical diagnosis of GIDC, but in less formal contexts ranging from homophobic bullying by peers and teachers and within the family to brutal chastisement and rape. Amnesty International and the UN Convention on the Rights of the Child both note that any violence against children and young people in the home or at school, including homophobic violence, not only damages the body, but has long-lasting and often devastating effects on the child's sense of dignity (AI 46). The victims of such stigmatization are seldom aware of it, since it is not of their making, and the shock of physical and/or psychic violence leaves them, initially at least, without an idiom to name it, and without the means of articulation and access to resist it. One must recall how long it took Jewish survivors of the Holocaust to break their silence and produce new idioms to name their experiences of Auschwitz and other death camps.

Since sexuality relates, as the Amnesty International report acknowledges, to the deepest affairs of the mind and the most intimate expressions of the body, same-sex desire, and its articulation and enactment, is ultimately connected, in the juridical sense, to the Universal Declaration of Human Rights and to the respect, integrity, and worth of the human person (7). Denying rights to a particular group undermines the entire framework of human rights for which fascism and nazism had no regard. Other forms of (homo)sexual oppression, which I do not have space to discuss in more detail here, remain in the contemporary world. For example, in April 2000 in Saudi Arabia, a judicial punishment of a flogging of up to 2,600 lashes each was handed down to nine young men with a prison term for "deviant sexual behavior." Under strict Islamic (*Shari'a*) law, this offense is related to other forms of consensual sex between adults which are believed to transgress religious or political codes, including any kind of sex outside the boundaries of conventional heterosexual marriage, and in some countries the *Shari'a* code provides for the death penalty for homosexuality (AI 19–20).

While received knowledge on sexual repression under the Third Reich points out that lesbians were not as systematically persecuted as were gay men, a point that I challenge in chapter 3, it must be kept in mind that the continuing effects of present-day oppression of those marked by sexual dissidence are by no means especially lenient to lesbians or to women in general. In many parts of the postcolonial world, women's sexuality and erotic expression are limited to marriage to a man within the same social community. Women who choose a marriage partner outside of what is arranged socially, or a partner outside of their ethnic, class, or religious boundaries, or women who have an erotic relationship with any man before or outside of marriage, or have an erotic relationship with another woman that excludes marriage to a man, are subject to degrading and violent treatment. Once again, as I noted in chapter 3, one must not only rely on the axis of sexuality alone in reading and understanding same-sex affective and erotic bonds between women (and the concomitant misogynistic and homophobic oppression), as the axis of gender must not be elided. Same-sex bonds between women in postcolonial and developing countries are placed under control and surveillance as part of the broader policing of women's sexuality by the family and by the larger community in more traditional societies, and women, whether or not they expressly define themselves as "lesbian," face an entirely different range of obstacles to erotic autonomy, resistance to oppression and violence, and the seeking of redress (AI 43–44) if they are found to desire women, especially in lieu of heterosexual marriage.

The power of dominant discourses and state apparatuses cannot be underestimated. In protest of a lesbian conference in Colombo, Sri Lanka, *The Island* newspaper, in a published letter in August 1999, asked for the police to "let loose convicted rapists among the jubilant but jaded jezebels … so that those who are misguided may get a taste of the real thing." When lesbians complained to the Sri Lankan Press Council, the Council refused to condemn the newspaper and replied that the view printed was justified given that lesbianism was an offense in the country's penal code (AI 43), thereby forming a link not only with what often happened to lesbians in the concentration camps where prisoners of war were ordered to "fuck them up good and proper," but also with the refusal of the German government to grant restitution to those interred in camps under Paragraph 175, since homosexuality was a crime before and during the nazi rise to power (and for a time afterward as discussed in the beginning of this chapter). The beating and raping of women found to be lesbian, or accused of it, were certainly coercive or "corrective" measures used in nazi camps, and many lesbians in various parts of the world today are forced into marriages or sexual relations with men, raped, and often subjected to forced virginity examinations by family members. Such asymmetrical expressions of violence and power within the domestic sphere, and such attempts by nation-states to support and condone the violent policing of female bodies, serve to reposition and naturalize heteronormativity and ensure its ideological longevity, which was similarly a goal of National Socialist policy.

Nazi homophobia, as I have argued throughout this book, was neither a momentary aberration nor a separate vector of power, since it occurred and was deeply embedded in material practices under specific sets of social, cultural, and ideological conditions. While the specific contexts of those conditions, such as racial hygiene, population politics, and fears of social and national degeneracy, have shifted since the time of National Socialism, they have by no means been eradicated entirely. In fact they have been refracted differentially under new sets of historical and political conditions in juridical law (especially through the effects of imperialism in the postcolonial world), medicine and psychiatry in the postwar years, and in the more recent diagnostic category of "Gender Identity Disorder in Childhood." These discursive traces of homophobia as socially situated and historically specific were especially prominent in the early days of the HIV/AIDS pandemic and continue in the ongoing global surveillance and tracking of HIV/AIDS by global health institutions worldwide, which rely on models of medicine and health care that reinvent a legacy of colonialism by viewing race and sexuality in hierarchical terms and by reifying, and thereby privileging, the positions of dominant races and classes in the West in terms of access to treatment and care. Moreover, the impact of these discursive traces, in addition to the day-to-day oppression that lesbians, gay men, and other sexual dissidents endure in various parts of the world, as Amnesty International has documented, is still very much tied to the systemic wish in culture, both under nazism and today, that gay people simply not exist. What might these connections and continuities, which are not straightforwardly traceable from nazism to the present, but nonetheless have continued to exist since the Third Reich, imply for the future?

6 | Queer Sexuality, Holocaust Studies, and the Challenge of Democratic Futurity

Making the politics of sexual difference more legible under the Third Reich while situating it at the nexus of other forms of nazi power, including race and anti-Semitism, gender norms, population politics, and eugenics, contributes to the ongoing question in Holocaust studies as to whether the Holocaust was a unique event in history or can also be compared to other genocides, genocidal tendencies, and state-sponsored forms of discrimination, victimization, and exclusion for purely ideological reasons. This latter part is important because, while no other group was as systematically murdered by the nazis as were Jewish victims, the seeds of the Final Solution for Jewish annihilation began in the virulent denial of human rights and legal protections to Jews and their gradual exclusion from deliberative participation in social life in Germany. Social prejudice and state hostility toward Jews and other racial groups, including Roma and Sinti, as Sybil H. Milton argues, had a long history in Germany and other parts of Europe long before the nazi assumption of power in 1933 (212–13). For this reason, it is important to acknowledge both the consequences of Third Reich power and its antecedents under the Weimar Republic and in the late nineteenth and early twentieth centuries, where theories of racial hygiene, eugenics, and "degeneration" had profound social influence up until the time of World War I and especially after Germany's defeat. Eugenicists and racial hygiene experts, according to Richard Evans, began to argue vehemently just after World War I for the idea of Nordic supremacy and its corollary view that Jews, Slavs, and other races were biologically inferior (32), and this was an important cultural precedent to nazi racial policy, which politicized and applied it not only to Jews but to other social groups who were thought to undermine Aryan racial purity.[1] The annihilation of Jews culminated in, and was refracted through, a history of material and ideological conditions in Germany and in Europe. Yet while the mechanisms of the Final Solution were aimed directly at Jews, knowledge of the strategies of social discrimination against other groups, including gay men and lesbians, contributes to a better understanding of National Socialism, even if the final figures for those exterminated or persecuted from other groups were nowhere near as high. The radicalization of anti-Semitism and the intensity of the marking of social outsiders under the Third Reich were ideologically connected to a massive reformulation of the idea of the German nation and its imperialist ambitions tied to the creation of a master race. But in pressing this specific goal further, distinctive nodes of social and cultural organization within National Socialism, and within present-day societies and cultures, are also made legible when we look closely at which groups are cast to the constitutive outside of formative discourses of national belonging. More generally, utopian ideas about material improvement and moral progress over time are challenged to the extent that they leave unexamined the power of political institutions, juridical and bureaucratic systems, and the social production of knowledge to define the limits of our existence—so much so, that, as Omer Bartov reminds us, "we enjoy our liberty and freedom as citizens of [so-called] western civilization with a sense of fear and foreboding" (91), and this has haunting implications for a post-Holocaust world.

Reading the Holocaust as a determinate object in history with a singular, static, or fixed meaning limits its significance and the ways in which it might be subject to a range of social, historical, and cultural questions. Ongoing interrogation of the Holocaust and its cultural meaning(s) does not automatically imply a fall down the very slippery slope of Holocaust denial, but is an attempt to locate a balance between remaining faithful to the historical evidence of the crimes of the nazis while, at the same time, being attentive to the blind spots, the gaps, the aporias of the historical record. Such questions perhaps could not have been asked earlier, given, for example, the fact that queer studies did not exist as a recognized discipline at the time that Holocaust studies became its own field of inquiry in the 1960s and a recognized academic discipline in the 1970s.[2] The evolution of the ongoing significance of the Holocaust has helped to create a space for the study of sexual difference as part of Holocaust inquiry, though historically the topic has not been treated seriously as Holocaust studies developed as a discipline. As Günter Grau argues, the topic of homosexuality and the Holocaust is still considered marginal in relation to the larger archive of research that addresses those persecuted for political, religious, or eugenic reasons ("Final Solution" 338).

There are many reasons for this marginalization. Researchers initially assumed that nazi persecutions against gay men were justifiable under Paragraph 175, which criminalized homosexuality; others believed that a focus on homosexuality would detract from the Judaic significance of the Holocaust. This book has argued that an analysis of sexuality is important to the overall study of the Holocaust and has attempted to situate the policing of sexual difference specifically within broader nazi social policies pertaining to eugenics, race, and population politics, while acknowledging that while desire is intimately felt, it is always already publicly mediated and cannot, therefore, be dismissed simply as a private matter with little or no social or historical significance.

Yet some reflections on the future of Holocaust studies express anxiety about the possible contamination of the "purity" of the Holocaust as a historical event and object of study through "Americanization," in Alvin Rosenfeld's usage of the term, implying a kind of vulgarization and crassness when social and political inquiries into the Holocaust are seen as acquiescing to the pressures of American identity politics.[3] But what must also be kept in mind is that, historically, research on the Holocaust has been bound to the kinds of questions researchers have wished to ask of its historical, cultural, and political significance. The study of the Holocaust and its representation in culture was rather sparse in the United States of the 1950s—a society that valued assimilation and consensus. Indeed, Hilene Flanzbaum reminds us that the 1960s and 1970s were eras more committed to diversity and ethnicity (black power, women's rights, etc.), and that the era helped to prompt an assertion and renewal of Jewish identity through the Holocaust (11) alongside other debates about ethnicity and oppression. In other words, cultural conditions and historical processes enabled the framing of questions around Jewish identity and history, which included the lived experience of the Holocaust by survivors, and the production of new knowledge about the Holocaust in a way similar to how more recent questions about sexuality have framed inquiry into the relationship between power and sexuality and the continued history of that relationship. Moreover, a fear that an analysis of sexual difference contaminates the "purity" of the Holocaust as a sacred object does not diminish its importance but broadens the sphere of inquiry. Tropes of purity and contamination not only attempt to foreclose discussion and debate on homophobia as a form of nazi power, but reinscribe the same tropes of purity, homogeneity, and contamination that similarly animated the nazi fascist gesture with regard to its racial policies.

One pertinent example of the shifting intellectual framework for understanding the Holocaust and the evolution of its social and cultural significance is *The Diary of Anne Frank*, perhaps one of the most widely read books on the Holocaust written from the perspective of one of its victims. As Flanzbaum argues, pointing to the *Diary*'s history and reception, the book went through numerous editions—from the original publication, where Otto Frank edited out material considered to be too personal or sexually suggestive (with altered or restored versions appearing in 1986, 1989, and 1991), to the *Definitive Edition of the Diary of Anne Frank* published in 1994—which revealed that earlier versions were adapted to fit the tastes of the reading public at the time and did not necessarily reveal the "truth" of the Holocaust or Anne's totalized experience of it. Rather, what analysis of the various versions shows, according to Flanzbaum, is that the earlier versions sugar-coated gruesome subject matter, and, along with the original stage and screen productions of the text in 1955 and 1959 respectively, played down Jewishness and tried to universalize Anne's experience under tropes of optimism, human dignity, and strength of spirit in the face of threat and deprivation (2–3). Instead of straightforwardly revealing any truth of the Holocaust, the editing of the original text by Otto Frank, and the original stage and screen productions, were very much tied to the social and historical context of assimilation and social conformity in the 1950s, especially in the American reception of Anne Frank's *Diary*. The history of the different versions of the book, as well as the history of its reception since its original publication, suggests that the meaning and significance of the Holocaust is not static or timeless, but that the Holocaust, as an ongoing "*image* and *symbol*, seems to have sprung loose from its origins," and its varied invocations become new intellectual sites for sifting, sorting, and analysis (Flanzbaum 8; emphasis added). This enables us to continually invoke new questions of the Holocaust while respecting its historical specificity.

The social, cultural, and historical significance of the Holocaust is not determined by received narratives alone that have rendered the Holocaust intelligible, but is also shaped by the kinds of questions researchers, historians, and cultural theorists wish to ask of it and its meaning. The posing of new questions through new frameworks has helped to create a space for the analysis of sexual difference as one possible lens for understanding this historical event. Indeed, even newer questions are being asked of *The Diary of Anne Frank* that compel us to read the desires of the young protagonist and narrator against the presupposed lens of heteronormativity and to consider the opening of a possible lesbian narrative space, as I discussed in chapter 3. At the same time, though, as I pointed out in chapter 1 and throughout this book, "queer" does not exist in particular bodies, identities, or acts alone (though it can address these), but as Sara Ahmed succinctly puts it, "queer" describes both a sexual and a political orientation that "unfolds from specific points, from the lifeworld of those who do not or cannot inhabit the contours of heterosexual space" (172). Yet, she continues, to lose sight of the sexual specificity of queer (alongside its intellectual and social functions as a mode of inquiry and as a site of social praxis) overlooks how heteronormativity shapes what coheres as given and the effects of this coherence on those who refuse to be so compelled (172), both of which, as I have tried to show in this book, have implications not only for gay men and lesbians who were persecuted by the nazis, and the various forms of oppression of sexual dissidents that have occurred since the end of World War II and into the present day, but for the researcher who wishes to read against the dominant grain of heterotextual narrative in an attempt to read what is, as Ahmed describes, "off line" (161), more literally, what is not "straight," in Holocaust research. A queer lens, or at least the way that I am attempting to use it here, is not merely a matter of including lesbians and gay men in dominant narratives of National Socialism and the Holocaust, but also operates hermeneutically to question strategies of representation and history that reinscribe sexual and textual normativities in the rendering of the Holocaust in the name of protecting its "originary" status, a status which is, in itself, a historical and social construction always already inscribed with a highly vested political point of view.

The orientation of perspective in Holocaust studies, then, traditionally has been one directed toward the heteronormative. In speaking about the process of becoming reorientated, of deviating from the paths one is supposed to follow, Ahmed also notes that through such alternative pathways one experiences a kind of disorientation, an encountering of the world differently, which is simultaneously a way of (re)constructing the world (19–20). While Ahmed is speaking more specifically about how lives and lived experiences get orientated or directed in some ways rather than in others, and in ways that are not necessarily casual or arbitrary (21), I am extending that here, and in this book in general, by arguing that the leaving of familiar "straight" paths and the formation of alternative lines in research and scholarship have had impact for new textual and intellectual pathways of inquiry in Holocaust studies. Not only can the direction of our gaze constitute our social world, as Ahmed notes, quoting Michael Warner (120),[4] but it can constitute new lines of knowledge production. This book has begun to develop these orientations and new directions further by not looking at sexual difference as a single intellectual pathway of inquiry alone, but through the ways in which it intersects and crosses at various points with race, nazi population politics, eugenics, gender, and other matrices through which the German Aryan and nationalist vision was socially shaped under National Socialism, thus demonstrating how an analysis of sexual difference deviates from the standard lines of inquiry in researching and teaching about the Holocaust while simultaneously enriching its study.

But challenging the mere assumption of heteronormativity is neither a task relegated to a re-seeing of the past, nor is it limited to raising implications for continuities in the present or to challenging received heterosexist perspectives in dominant interpretations of the Holocaust, but resurfaces, perhaps more covertly, in terms of new visions (queer) scholarship articulates for a post-Holocaust world. In other words, there is a not-yet-theorized insistence in most Holocaust scholarship that the dissemination of its findings will be passed on to younger generations as a safeguard against future forms of genocide and intolerance through the knowledge gained about the victims and survivors of nazi atrocities. While Holocaust scholarship and its dissemination are crucially important, given historical elisions, denials, and silences, especially in the years immediately following World War II, there has also been a politics of remembrance since the time Holocaust scholarship began to get seriously underway in the 1960s and 1970s, wherein certain groups, such as homosexuals, were not recognized as victims, as I've already discussed in the previous chapter. But more important, appeals to the efficacy of Holocaust research for the future rest on a rather shaky faith in history as linear progression and can instantiate an ideology of reproductive futurism, which Lee Edelman refers to as the absolute privilege of heteronormativity as an organizing principle of communal relations that is authenticated and transmitted to the future through the figure of the Child. In fact, in Edelman's view, the rhetorical appeal to the figure of the Child helps structure the entire logic in which the political (i.e., heteropatriarchal) must be thought (*No Future* 2–3) while guaranteeing its ideological longevity.[5]

Now by writing this, I am not suggesting that there is something ignoble about the social and political implications of Holocaust research for imagining a better future and learning about the atrocities of suffering and violence, especially given continued forms of intolerance such as racism, homophobia, misogyny, xenophobia, and genocide since the time of the Holocaust. Any kind of theorizing, queer or otherwise, cannot simply turn a blind eye to the materialities of human suffering in the name of intellectual pursuit or critique; otherwise, in critiquing one form of normativity we leave others unexamined, and this has been a critique of queer theory's anti-relational thesis, which was first formulated by Leo Bersani in his book *Homos*. While I agree with Bersani's observation of "the rage for respectability so visible in gay life today," to the extent that he is referring to the present and to the West, his question "Should a homosexual be a good citizen?" and his challenge to "the compatibility of homosexuality with civic service" (113) resonates a bit differently when we shift the context to other locations. For example, lesbians and gay men in much of the postcolonial world do hope to be good citizens while helping to transform discursive strands of cultural nationalism in many postcolonial nation-states that insist that homosexuality is alien to its indigenous traditions. This was particularly evidenced by the work of queer activism in South Africa in the immediate aftermath of apartheid in the early 1990s to ensure the insertion of a constitutional clause that expressly prohibited discrimination on the basis of sexual orientation. The clause eventually enabled the complete decriminalization of homosexuality in South Africa in 1998. For many sexual dissidents in the postcolonial and Third Worlds, economic conditions may make western queer opposition to community seem a western luxury. Certainly, those ravaged by HIV/AIDS in South Africa and other parts of sub-Sahara Africa do hope for, and try to imagine, a better future—even the mere possibility of a future—as a strategy for survival. Their hope endures despite the fact that access to prevention programs and anti-retroviral medication was prevented by the combination of misunderstandings of African sexuality by global health organizations, initial denials of the dangers of an HIV epidemic in South Africa by the government in the 1980s, racist stereotypes proffered by western pharmaceutical companies that poor indigenous Africans, the most endangered group, lacked the literacy skills necessary to take the regimen of prescribed drugs responsibility, and continued denials by President Thabo Mbeki regarding the efficacy of anti-retroviral therapy.[6] Local AIDS activists in South Africa, as well as organizations such as *Médecins sans Frontières* (MSF), are highly invested in Africa's future in their work to pressure the South African government to make anti-retroviral medication more accessible to those living with HIV/AIDS and in their efforts to import less costly generic versions of patented anti-retroviral drugs for the treatment of HIV infection. Such activist work has helped life-saving drugs reach those who are suffering with HIV/AIDS in South Africa, whether through the national health care system or in treatment programs of the MSF in impoverished townships.[7]

Of course, such work may be small-scale and may not be enough to end the AIDS pandemic. But, at the same time, not all visions of community and articulations of a better future are proffered in the name of reproductive futurity and can offer the potential for social change. While queerness may never be fully compatible with social respectability, and indeed may sometimes be productively regarded as "the side of those *not* 'fighting for the children,' the side outside the consensus by which all politics confirms the absolute value of reproductive futurism" (Edelman, *No Future* 3), it may be more productive to rethink articulated visions of the future rather than to dismiss them and all communal and social relations as always already implicated in heteronormativity in the same way. "Queer," as a mode of analysis and as a strategy of opposition, makes little sense unless it is understood relationally; its highly contested identities and its political practices are always already positioned, socially and discursively, in relation with/to others.[8] In speaking of lesbian struggles for erotic autonomy in the Bahamas—where the 1991 Sexual Offences and Domestic Violence Act simultaneously criminalized lesbian sex and restricted legal recourse for married women who were domestically abused by their husbands—M. Jacqui Alexander asks the compelling question as to whether it is possible to imagine a feminist emancipatory project "in which women can love themselves, love women, and transform the nation simultaneously" ("Erotic Autonomy" 100). There may be something quite Eurocentric, and rather imperialist, in the valorization of queer as anti-relational to the extent that many sexual dissidents in the developing world, while certainly influenced in varying degrees by western queer activism, do not wish merely to imitate western notions of queer insofar as they may be heavily invested in the differences of their cultural identities and their indigenous cultural histories, and, in the case of the "New" South Africa, their hope for the possibilities of social transformation since apartheid and in the midst of the AIDS pandemic. Given a history of colonialism and continued forms of economic imperialism that contribute to the peripherization of Africa, the articulation of a hope for the future and a better vision of communal relations is by no means frivolous or naively utopian, but speaks to western queer theory's elitist impulses if it simply dismisses such articulated hopes as such.

At the same time, it is important to be self-reflexive in terms of the visions of the future we articulate to the extent that appeals to futurity may remain heavily ensconced in heteronormative frames of reference, reinventing new sites of social and epistemological exclusion centered largely on the cult of the traditional family. And, in another deployment of heteronormative power, those who refuse this insistence and investment in the regime of reproductive futurity are marked as irresponsible or as inhumane (Edelman, *No Future* 4). The nazis themselves were heavily invested—indeed obsessed—with reproductive futurity and the image of the Child through the politics of race and racial hygiene, eugenics, and gender (given that "distinguished" citizens, that is, normative Aryan Germans, were marked from mere inhabitants, such as unmarried and childless women and non-Aryans under the Citizenship Law of 1935, which similarly deprived Jews of all civil rights and liberties).[9] To what extent does the reliance on, and the invocation of, reproductive futurism in Holocaust scholarship, captured in the image of the Child, continue to reproduce a stigmatized otherness as a threat (read: queer in its broadest antinormative stance) to the very protection of the regime of reproductive futurity in the contemporary world? To what extent is non-reproductive eros in Holocaust scholarship left in the lurch, given that the nazis saw homosexuality as a threat to the Aryan race, as the placement of individual pleasure above the needs of the nation-state, as outside of the norms of gender for its citizens, and as a crime under the Reich Penal Code? And to what extent has Holocaust scholarship continued to leave homosexuality in the lurch, given its historical marginalization of gay and lesbian victims and its resistance to queer (re)readings?

While it is important to recognize the ways in which Holocaust scholarship may be somewhat invested discursively in a regime of reproductive futurity, this cannot signal an impasse but must produce new sites of dissidence and deliberation in research, in the academy, and in the public sphere. The Holocaust, as stated at the beginning of this chapter, is not merely a fixed event in time; its significance is shaped by historical sources as well as by the kinds of questions we as researchers wish to ask of it. As Michael R. Marrus observes:

> Fundamentally what keeps the subject [of the Holocaust] alive as an intellectual discourse is that the itch to understand is a never-ending process. So long as our historical culture is pluralistic and open, so long as our intellectual life is free and challenging, new questions will rain down on Holocaust history. Count on the next generation to frame different problems even for the sources we have already examined.... They will have their own historiographical controversies, their own perplexities, and the day may even come when they will wonder why we even bothered with our own quarrels of any given moment. (33–34)

Though Marrus's statement may seem to be caught up in a politics of futurity and hope, it would be naïve to dismiss it completely, because it does help to create an intellectual and political space for the theorization of sexual difference within Holocaust inquiry. More important, it recognizes that social relations are often in conflict and incite discursive practices of disagreement and negotiation based on rhetorical practices of civic engagement that urge a point of view to be taken and argued. Hence researchers interested in engaging sexual difference as a mode of inquiry into the Holocaust are interpellated into this very discursive space of negotiation at the very moment that they take up the question of sexual difference. Marrus is not implying that new ideas about the Holocaust are a mere collection of whatever is said about it under some banner of free speech and free inquiry, but is suggesting instead that well-thought-out and carefully researched ideas about the Holocaust and its significance, which include questions of sexuality and sexual difference, are connected to historical processes that enable the asking of new kinds of questions and debating them with and against ideas that have already been established. Speaking to the interdependence of rhetorical democracy and civic engagement, Gerard Hauser explains that the expression of oppositional points of view in the public sphere does not imply that those who are in disagreement will find opposing points of view as acceptable as their own, but that they will engage with, and respond to, them as legitimate contributions to the deliberative process (9). This is especially needed in Holocaust studies in terms of how we deliberate in print and in the public domain, given a history of chauvinism that has prevented new forms of inquiry from being heard, particularly those pertaining to gender and sexuality. This was certainly the case in the symposium on gender and the Holocaust to which I referred at the very beginning of this book. Historians of sexuality are now beginning to use old sources to pose new questions, so much so that, as Elizabeth Heineman argues, the persecution of sexual minorities under National Socialism and nazi efforts to control reproduction are perhaps beginning to be no longer seen as marginal to nazi racial theory and practice, but are gradually coming to be regarded as quite central (65–66).[10]

Moreover, one catalyst for shaping new questions about the Holocaust is the impact of social injustices in the present age and the rethinking of history as linear, anticipatory progression. We may wish to begin with knowledge production itself: How is it derived from our theoretical orientations about the world and our understanding about how history is made? As M. Jacqui Alexander envisions, in speaking of a collective feminist vision of justice that takes into account the effects of imperialism on women in the postcolonial world, we can then ask how justice should be practiced and begin to imagine new modes of living and being that support that vision. Alexander isn't merely advocating an appeal to futurity in the name of future generations or in the name of the Child, but is insisting on a radical re-examination and transformation of *inherited* practices, both social and intellectual, that may stand in the way of justice (*Pedagogies of Crossing* 92–93). For instance, the long-term refusal of western pharmaceutical companies to make anti-retroviral drugs available to indigenous Africans infected with HIV, which would have saved many more lives, was not the result of homophobia or racism alone (though those vectors of power were obviously there as they were in the early days of the pandemic in the West when medical communities and politicians reacted to the threat of HIV/AIDS with indifference, as I discussed in chapter 5), but was an instance, as Alexander phrases it, in which capitalism frustrated democracy, how the imperatives of the so-called free-market economy stood in the way of justice (*Pedagogies* 92). We cannot, therefore, see the Holocaust merely as a discrete event in history, but must theorize radically its continued significance in the everyday world.

Postcolonial women of color, given the history of the exploitation of their labor and their bodies under colonialism and the postcolonial nation-state, as well as by the transnational and multinational corporations who employ them locally, know that imperialism was not a momentary event in history, with discrete boundaries neatly relegated to the period of territorial occupation by colonial rule. Rather, the entire history of colonialism has undergone a series of shifts, and what this implies of history in general, according to Alexander, is that it always already proceeds in a way that makes ruptures and bland forms of periodization (like the problematic "post" in "postcolonial) seem neither clear-cut nor final because of the ongoing persistence of imperialist tendencies coming from the West and from postcolonial continuities that remain after colonial occupation and rule (*Pedagogies* 93). To what extent is the continued criminalization of homosexuality in many parts of the world, the refusal to see the rights of sexual dissidents as human rights, and the stigmatization of suffering that comes with HIV/AIDS indicative of the nation-state's propensity toward violence in the name of nation building, sovereignty, and decolonization? Imperialist impulses are not only refracted through postcolonial nation-states, but were similarly evident in nationalistic and global tropes of defense and protection manufactured by the United States to garner patriotic support as it prepared for the military invasion of Iraq. This was very much gendered, as Alexander notes, through the idea that the superior might of white western masculinity, as defender of the globe, would vanquish orientalist masculinity, the enemy of the globe—Saddam Hussein—playing on stereotypes of the treacherous and cruel Arab/Muslim other, whom it had become culturally legitimate to hate (*Pedagogies* 96).[11] Yet the tinge of homophobia is not altogether absent in the feminization and othering of Saddam Hussein and orientalist masculinity, since the very gendering sets up Hussein in particular—and Arab/Islamic masculinity in general—as enemies of a globalized world through the racialization of gender and sexuality. What might this signify in a post-Holocaust world? Are the power differentials (between those of the past and those of the present) really all that dissimilar? Must we necessarily declare an end to strategies of power that continue to be deployed in ways that survive the era to which they have been assigned temporally in the annals of history?

Struggles for erotic autonomy, then, are not simply restricted to other times and places. Nor are they merely trivial or reducible to the private domain to the extent that, as Dagmar Herzog notes in her book *Sex after Fascism*, struggles over sexuality are inflected with conflicts over other relations of power and provide us with profound opportunities to think about the workings of ideologies (not only sexual ideologies) and how they take hold of individuals and constitute subjectivities and possibilities for resistance (261). The politics of sexual difference, then, serves as a useful lens, alongside others, with which to analyze power under the Third Reich, broaden the scope of Holocaust studies, and deepen the meaning of the Holocaust both as a historical event and in its ongoing significance. But at the same time, sexuality, as a legitimate axis of theoretical and historical inquiry in the study of the Holocaust, can provide one possible organizing framework, one interface always interlocking with others, as to the ways in which social worlds are historically shaped and socially invented. Moreover, queer theory as a hermeneutic tool can enable continued, yet perhaps more oblique, pathways of deliberation on the paradox of modernity, always already caught between social progress on the one hand and regression through brutal violence on the other, the latter of which (violence) is often justified in the name of the former (progress), as it was under the Third Reich, and has remained long after. . . .

Notes

Introduction

1. See Omer Bartov, "Kitsch and Sadism in Ka-Tzetnik's Other Planet: Israeli Youth Imagine the Holocaust," *Jewish Social Studies* 3.2 (1997): 42–76.
2. See Dirk Blasius, "Das Ende der Humanität: Psychiatrie und Krankenmord in der NS-Zeit," *Der historiche Ort des Nationalsozialismus*, ed. Walter Pehle (Frankfurt: S. Fischer Verlag, 1990), 52.
3. I am referring here more to nationalist discourses in South Africa historically, especially during the apartheid era when homosexuality was criminalized through the Immorality Act of 1957, which later became the Sexual Offences Act and criminalized a range of nonheteronormative forms of sexuality and any form of interracial sex during the marked social trend of sexual policing in South Africa during the 1950s and 1960s. This trend of criminalization continued with the Immorality Amendment Act (Act 57 of 1969), which raised the age of consent for homosexual sex from sixteen to nineteen, and Schedule One of the Criminal Procedure Act of 1977, which allowed for the arrest of any person "reasonably" suspected of having committed sodomy. But even in the "New" South Africa of the post-apartheid period, some strands of African cultural nationalism interpreted homosexuality as a vestige of empire and as alien to African indigenous cultures. This was especially evident in the defense trial of Winnie Madikizela Mandela in 1991 when she was accused of taking part in the abductions, and possibly the beatings, of four black youths who were supposedly being abused sexually by a white Methodist minister. Many of her supporters defended her actions, carrying placards reading "Homosex is not in black culture" outside the courthouse during her trial in the same year that the ANC had formalized its commitment to equal rights for gays and lesbians in the draft Bill of Rights, which eventually appeared

in the country's new Constitution. Appeals to nationalism and to homosexuality as contrary to African indigenous cultures remained long after apartheid and also appeared in neighboring countries, such as in Zimbabwe in recent tirades against homosexuality by President Robert Mugabe, and in speeches by President Sam Nujoma of Namibia, one of which articulated homosexuality as a "national threat" in 2001. See Spurlin, *Imperialism within the Margins*, especially chapter 4, for further discussion.

4 Quoted from Claudia Schoppmann, *Days of Masquerade* 18; see also nazi women's book, 1934, cited in Westenreider, "*Deutsche Frauen und Mädchen!*" 47.

1 Holocaust Studies Meets Queer Studies: A Contested Alliance?

1 See work such as Heinz Heger's *The Men with the Pink Triangle: The True Life-and-Death Story of Homosexuals in the Nazi Death Camps* (1980); Richard Plant, *The Pink Triangle: The Nazi War Against Homosexuals* (1986); Claudia Schoppmann, *Days of Masquerade: Life Stories of Lesbians During the Third Reich* (1996; originally published in German as *Zeit der Maskierung: Lebensgeschichten lesbischer Frauen im "Dritten Reich,"* 1993); Pierre Seel, *Liberation Was for Others: Memoirs of a Gay Survivor of the Nazi Holocaust* (1997; originally published in French as *Moi, Pierre Seel, deporté homosexuel*, 1994); and Gad Beck, *An Underground Life: Memoirs of a Gay Jew in Nazi Berlin* (1999), to name a few of these early memoirs.

2 See Raul Hilberg's book *The Destruction of the European Jews*, rev. ed., 3 vols., New York: Holmes, 1985, as noted in Hirsch and Kacandes. Also see Hirsch and Kacandes for a short history of the development of courses in Holocaust studies in the late 1960s and 1970s (5–6).

3 See chapter 5 for a full discussion of these issues, especially the history of homosexuality as a diagnostic category in the different editions of the *Diagnostic and Statistical Manual of Mental Disorders* (*DSM*) published by the American Psychiatric Association, the representation of homosexuality as alien to indigenous cultures in some postcolonial contexts, the globalization of AIDS discourses worldwide, which still points to economic unevenness in terms of access to drugs and treatment, and the stigma of homosexuality and HIV/AIDS in poorer countries of the world.

4 Given historical elisions and erasures regarding gay men and lesbians as Holocaust victims, research in this area must still account for the specificity of gay and lesbian identities under National Socialism and not deny the historical fact of their persecution, arrest, internment in camps, torture, subjection to medical experimentation, physical/mental abuse in camps, murder and extermination, difficulties encountered by those who survived to reintegrate into postwar society without being recognized as victims of nazi atrocities, and, for some, additional persecution after the war as criminals, since homosexuality remained in the German Penal Code until 1969 in the former West Germany.

This acknowledgment does not necessarily mean an essentialization of gay or lesbian identity, nor does it imply a reduction of identity to one's sexuality alone. It is rather an attempt to insert lesbian and gay subject positions more meaningfully into scholarship on the Third Reich and the Holocaust as a way of broadening understandings of the relationship between sexuality and power and to account for the interimplication of sexuality in other forms of social discrimination and disenfranchisement.

5 Paragraph 175 criminalized homosexuality but was revised in 1935 (Paragraph 175A) so that criminal persecution need not be based on simply being caught in the sex act with another man, but could also include the abuse of relations of dependence based on employment, service, and subordination by the mere proposition that sex between men occur. Men could be liable for homosexual prosecution for the expression of desire for another man (love letters, verbal expression), and any kind of male-male physical contact that could be read as homoerotic or sexual. This is more specifically discussed in the following chapter, and the ramifications of lesbian sex not being written into the Reich Penal Code and its revision are discussed in chapter 3. Though lesbian sex was neither explicitly written into Paragraph 175, nor written into its subsequent revision, women could be, and sometimes were, prosecuted under similar grounds.

6 See Spurlin, *Imperialism within the Margins* 136–39, and Hema Chari's essay "Colonial Fantasies and Postcolonial Identities."

7 As Foucault writes: "The nineteenth-century homosexual became a personage, a past, a case history, and a childhood, in addition to being a type of life, a life form, and a morphology, with an indiscreet anatomy and possibly a mysterious physiology.... Homosexuality appeared as one of the forms of sexuality when it was transposed from the practice of sodomy onto a kind of interior androgyny, a hermaphrodism of the soul. The sodomite had been a temporary aberration; the homosexual was now a species" (*History of Sexuality* 43). While this passage is often seen as controversial historically and culturally, and while I have critiqued Foucault myself for not accounting for the impact of colonialism and its racialization of sexuality, which locates his theory and history of sexuality more firmly in the West (see note 6 above), I use Foucault's discussion of this shift in understanding homosexuality as an emergent identic category (as opposed to its earlier status) in order to qualify sexuality as a discursive and cultural production, which is necessary to an understanding of homosexuality under nazism.

8 However, the focus has changed somewhat in recent years, thanks to the important work of Dagmar Herzog and other scholars discussed in the introduction to this book who attempt to theorize sexuality as deeply intertwined with nazi power. See Herzog; Gregor, Roemer, and Roseman; and Heineman, for example. The present book, however, is specifically concerned with a theorization of sexual difference as a way of making it more legible under the Third Reich at the nexus of other forms of nazi power and social policy, and as a way of making the politics of sexual difference more legible in Holocaust studies so as to open up new pathways of inquiry and new thinking about the ongoing cultural significance of the Holocaust.

9 Most interesting, under imperialism, homosexuality practiced by indigenous African men was not tolerated and more severely punished if it occurred interracially, as has been supported by court records in colonial Rhodesia. For further discussion of this, see Marc Epprecht, *Hungochani: The History of a Dissident Sexuality in Southern Africa*, chapter 4, especially pp. 129–130.

10 For examples of the reduction of homosexuality to a European phenomenon in southern Africa, see Spurlin, *Imperialism within the Margins*; in India, see Ruth Vanita, *Queering India: Same-Sex Love and Eroticism in Indian Culture and Society*; and in the Caribbean, see M. Jacqui Alexander, "Erotic Autonomy as a Politics of Decolonization: An Anatomy of Feminist and State Practice in the Bahamas Tourist Economy" in M. Jacqui Alexander and Chandra Talpade Mohanty (eds), *Feminist Genealogies, Colonial Legacies, Democratic Futures*.

11 I realize, of course, from work by Gayatri Spivak and others that any construction of the so-called subaltern voice is at best an imperial fantasy, that is, always already constructed by hegemonic voices (Spivak ix–x), given the positioning of postcolonial studies (and queer studies) in the western academy. My purpose is not to bring sexuality to the center of postcolonial studies, the history of the Third Reich, or Holocaust studies, but to interrogate nationalism from another angle so as to help open up and articulate overlooked axes of heterogeneity and difference in German nationalism under the Third Reich, in prevailing historical scholarship on the period, and in Holocaust scholarship.

2 The Racialization of Sexuality: Rethinking Same-Sex Desire within Nazi Juridical Discourse

1 These examples are not intended, of course, to be exhaustive. Rather, I am interested in looking at alternative trajectories to understand the various Holocaust victims rather than depending on the Jewish/non-Jewish split. I am grateful to Gordon C. Zahn for the categorization in his chapter "Pacifists During the Third Reich" in Berenbaum. See p. 194.

2 See also Herbert Marcuse, *Technology, War and Fascism: Collected Papers of Herbert Marcuse, Vol. 1*, ed. Douglas Kellner (New York: New York University Press, 1998).

3 Paragraph 175A also indicated that the male who perpetrated the sex offence could either be in the more active position or "allow himself to be abused for a sex offence" in each of the instances mentioned in the text above. However, whether the perpetrator played the more active or passive role sexually does not indicate that the law was speaking only of anal or oral penetration, intercrural sex, or self-gratification, which was the focus of the earlier law.

4 Lauding the revision of Paragraph 175, one nazi official commented that the change filled a gap in the law, since the earlier version only applied to "intercourse-like sex acts" that required police and public prosecutors to prove that such acts had in fact occurred. The official, an assistant department head at the Reich Ministry of Justice, points to the fact that a wider range of sex offenses, rather than specific intercourse-like acts occurring between men, could make homosexuals liable for imprisonment under the criminal code. See Grau, excerpt from details of the amendment of June 28, 1935, to the criminal law in *Hidden Holocaust?* pp. 66–67.

5 These debates are discussed at length, along with a further analysis of gender in relation to lesbian subject positions under National Socialism, in the next chapter.

6 This quotation is taken from the Guidelines of the Kassel Police Authority for combating homosexuality and abortion as laid out by Himmler and institutionalized in the Reichszentrale zur Bekämpfung der Homosexualität und der Abtreibung, to be discussed shortly. The memo referred to here (May 11, 1937), translated by Grau, goes on to list practical ways of implementing Himmler's directives.

7 The Röhm Purge refers to the June 30, 1934, murder of SA (*Sturmabteilung* or nazi storm trooper) leader Ernst Röhm, who was homosexual. By being openly homosexual, Röhm presented a conflict within the Nazi Party, since it advocated the prosecution of homosexuality. Initially Röhm was defended by Hitler insofar as the SA was necessary for the nazis to seize and maintain power, and some sources have indicated that the murders of Röhm and others in the so-called purge were politically motivated so that Hitler could consolidate power and his role as Führer. But in the murder of Röhm in particular, as Stefan Micheler argues, homophobia was exploited by showing Röhm as disloyal, forming a homosexual clique to subvert the state, which was later used to justify the persecution of homosexuals on the grounds of disloyalty, subversion, etc. (106–7). Yet most sources do agree that the Röhm assassination marked a decisive turn in the intolerance of homosexuality within the nazi ranks and in general.

8 See Sander Gilman's *Difference and Pathology: Stereotypes of Sexuality, Race, and Madness* for further discussion of this point.

9 Mosse states that the opportunity for homosexuals to reform, an option not available to Jews, through discipline and hard labor, was not given to congenital homosexuals (about 2 percent of men found guilty of homosexual acts and whose homosexuality was thought to be biologically or genetically based), as they were to be exterminated (*Nationalism and Sexuality* 143). Also in his Bad Tölz speech in November 1937, Himmler claimed that homosexuality was acquired through a lack of feminine contact, and once homosexuals were more systematically persecuted and put in concentration camps, many were exterminated if they were found unable to perform sexually with a woman, usually a camp prostitute.

10 Prior to the establishment of the Central Reich Office for Combating Homosexuality and Abortion in 1936, a special department of the Secret State Police Bureau began the

task of registering and prosecuting homosexuals as early as 1934, as Wolfgang Röll notes (9), until Himmler expanded this authority to the newly created Reichszentrale.

11 Himmler's secret directive of October 10, 1936, that sets up the Central Reich Office for Combating Homosexuality and Abortion reads as follows:

Die erhebliche Gefährdung der Bevölkerungspolitik und Volksgesundheit durch die auch heute noch verhältnismäßig hohe Zahl von Abtreibungen, die einen schweren Verstoß gegen die weltanschaulichen Grundsätze des Nationalsozialismus darstellen sowie die homosexuelle Betätigung einer nicht unerheblichen Schicht der Bevölkerung, in der eine der großten Gefahren für die Jugend liegt, erfordert mehr als bisher eine wirksame Bekämpfung dieser Volksseuchen.

1. Die Bearbeitung der obenangeführten Delikte liegt grundsätzlich der örtlich zuständigen Kriminalpolizei ob.
2. Um eine zentrale Erfassung und eine wirksame Bekämpfung dieser Vergehen nach einheitlichen Richtlinien sicherzustellen, errichte ich beim Preußischen Landeskriminalpolizeiamt eine Reichszentrale zur Bekämpfung der Homosexualität und der Abtreibung.

(qtd. in Grau, *Hidden Holocaust?* 89)

[The serious danger to population policy and public health represented by the still relatively high number of abortions which are a major violation of the worldview of National Socialism, as well as homosexual activity by a considerable segment of the population, which poses one of the greatest dangers to youth, requires more than ever before the effective combating of these public scourges.

1. The handling of the above offenses is essentially the responsibility of local police.
2. In order to ensure standard guidelines for central registration for the combating of these offenses, I establish within the Prussian Land Criminal Police Bureau a Central Reich Office for the Combating of Homosexuality and Abortion.]

12 The report indicates that 9,081 homosexual men were sentenced in 1936, 12,760 in 1937, 10,628 in 1938, and 10,450 in 1939; totalling 42,919 for this period (Plant 231).

13 These figures are from Micheler's examination of records of the Hamburg District Court, some of which were destroyed. See Micheler 126–27n.

14 Mosse here is citing Johann Valentin Müller's *The Outline of Forensic Medicine* (1796), in which Müller attempted to describe the outward signs of homosexuality (reddened eyes, feebleness, fits of depression, negligence about personal appearance) so that "perverts" could be caught, tried, and sentenced in courts. Müller had also written that masturbation could lead to homosexuality (an idea later supported by R. von Krafft-Ebing) and, according to Mosse, many of Müller's arguments resurfaced in the nineteenth century as justification for the punishment of so-called sexual abnormalities. See Mosse, *Nationalism and Sexuality* 29. But, at the same time, other

work has suggested that sexual repression was only one aspect of nazi sexual ideology and that the nazis also encouraged sexual experimentation and pre- and extra-marital sex, as well as other outlets for sexual pleasure beyond marriage for heterosexual Aryans (i.e., those who were not in groups persecuted by the nazis) as a way of increasing population growth, a point to which I shall return later.

15 *Das Schwarze Korps*, an official journal of the SS (*Schutzstaffeln* or elite nazi corps of guard detachments), printed weekly, supported such sexual practices as masturbation, non-procreative sexual pleasure within marriage, extra-marital heterosexual sex, etc., as "life-affirming," while attacking Jews, homosexuals, the handicapped, and critics of the regime as degenerate. The journal also attacked the unnaturalness of sexual prudery in heterosexual relations and mocked Catholic dogma to protect the sanctity of marriage (Herzog, "Hubris and Hypocrisy" 10–11; see also *Das Schwarze Korps*, June 19, 1935 and April 16, 1936).

16 Brand also published the journal *Der Eigene*, which appeared in different forms and in shifting political tones from 1896 to 1931. The group was inspired by romantic views of *Kultur* that regarded the priority of aesthetic and spiritual values rooted in the German soul (Oosterhuis, "Male Bonding" 242).

17 See Hirschfeld's "Die objecktive Diagnose der Homosexualität" in *Jahrbuch für sexuelle Zwischenstufen* (1899).

18 Much has already been written on the homoerotic appeal of National Socialism under nazi rule. For example, Mosse writes of how German nationalism celebrated the powerfully built, masculine nude male as representative of the strength of the nation and how fascism in general grafted homoeroticism onto the surfaces of its national symbols. See Mosse, *Nationalism and Sexuality*, chapter 8. Also see Klaus Theweleit's analysis of the male soldier in *Male Fantasies, Vol.2. Male Bodies: Psychoanalyzing the White Terror* in chapter 1, especially pp. 142–76. I will discuss this more fully in chapter 4. The homoerotic appeal of the nazis is not really my point in this work as much as the role of male bonding as a strategy of power in relation to the maintenance of male domination and population policy (tied to the erotic autonomy of men) and as a weakening of family life in contradiction to nazi propaganda aimed at protecting it from groups who posed a threat to the family, a point to which I have already alluded and one to which I shall shortly return.

19 The rhetoric of disavowal is not peculiar to nazi ideals of male comradeship and is also evident in contemporary arguments in keeping gays out of the military (or, in the case of the U.S. military, keeping gay men in the closet through its "Don't ask, don't tell, don't pursue" policy), and out of other homosocial organizations such as the Boy Scouts of America (BSA). The BSA has a national policy that homosexuality is not consistent with the obligations of scouting, and this was supported by the U.S. Supreme Court in June 2000 in its overturning of a court order by the New Jersey Supreme Court forbidding discrimination on the basis of sexual orientation within the BSA.

20 This is not to assume that the hypermasculinity projected by nazism was straightforwardly or self-evidently reducible to latent homosexuality, a point I shall take up in chapter 4. Also, the importance of understanding same-sex desire within nazi ideologies of gender is further developed in the next chapter; without a sufficient analysis of gender, I argue, lesbians are rendered potentially invisible under National Socialism.

21 For further discussion of this point, see Jonathan Friedman's *Speaking the Unspeakable: Essays on Sexuality, Gender and Holocaust Survivor Memory*, especially chapter 1: The "Eugenic Utopia," pp. 22–25.

22 Brutal treatment, as well as the varied kinds of same-sex relations within camps such as Buchenwald, the extermination camp with the highest proportion of homosexual inmates, is described in more detail in testimonies. See, for example, Heger, *The Men with the Pink Triangle*; Seel, *Liberation Was for Others: Memoirs of a Gay Survivor of the Nazi Holocaust*; and van Dijk, *La déportation des homosexuels: Onze témoignages: Allemagne 1933–1945*.

3 The Politics of Gender Difference: Lesbian Existence under the Third Reich

1 See Joan Miriam Ringelheim, "The Holocaust: Taking Women into Account," *Jewish Quarterly* (Autumn 1992): 22.

2 I am using the term "lesbian existence" in the sense used by Adrienne Rich in her essay "Compulsory Heterosexuality and Lesbian Existence" that accounts for the existence of lesbians across diverse historical periods and socio-geographical locations in spite of dominant discourses that try to erase it or render it unimaginable. Closely related to her notion of lesbian existence, and as a way of differentiating it from gay men, Rich refers to the lesbian continuum as a *range* of woman-identified experiences through specific women's lives and throughout history and "not simply the fact that a woman has had or consciously desired genital sexual experience with another woman" ("Compulsory Heterosexuality and Lesbian Existence" 51). Granted there are controversies surrounding Rich's notion of a lesbian continuum, particularly since many lesbians have argued that it obliterates the specificity of women who relate erotically to other women and fails to differentiate them from those who simply form close emotional bonds with women. Yet I still believe that Rich's notion of lesbian existence is useful here to begin to theorize a much-overlooked space within the domain of Holocaust scholarship. Thus, I use the term more as a discursive and political opening, as well as a conceptual space, contextualized by the historical and social specificities of the nazi period.

3 See Hirschfeld's preface to Roellig. He specifically notes: "Mit der vorliegenden kleinen Schrift wird der Versuch unternommen, die Allgemeinheit in leichtverständlicher Weise vertraut zu machen mit dem Vorhandensein jener Frauen, die nur zum gleichen

Geschlecht Liebe empfinden.... Das Buch verfolgt in erster Linie den Zweck, der breiten Öffentlichkeit Aufklärung zu bringen über die Wesensart, den Charakter und die Gewohnheiten dieser Menschengruppe, teils um tiefeingewurzelte Vorurteile auszurotten" (Hirschfeld; qtd. in Roellig 10).

4 Hirschfeld states: "Um Verständnis und Duldung wollen diese Zeilen werben für jene Menschen, Frauen, die ebensowenig als krank, minderwertig, wie unsittlich oder gar als verbrecherisch anzusehen sind" (Hirschfeld; qtd. in Roellig 12). Roellig, in the French version of her main text, writes: "Il suffit de se référer aux écrits du célèbre sexologue, le Docteur Magnus Hirschfeld. Cela m'évitera de me perdre en détails. Mais on ne pourra jamais assez répéter la chose suivante, à savoir que les lesbiennes ne sont ni malades, ni inférieures. Elles sont certes différentes, mais de valeur égale aux êtres normaux, et souvent dotées d'une grande intelligence et de dons artistiques" (23).

5 "The general characterization male/female is simply not sufficient.... Among all living organisms, the intermediary sexual stages are perfectly normal; far from being pathological, their appearance in no way signifies bodily or physical decadence" (my translation).

6 See Eberhard 559 and Schoppmann, *Days of Masquerade* 6. But the views expressed by Eberhard, and certainly echoed by his other contemporaries under the Weimar who similarly advocated for the inclusion of lesbian sex under Paragraph 175, did not represent a consensus against female homosexuality in Germany later under National Socialism, as analysis of transcripts of nazi debates on the subject show. I will take up this point later.

7 The 1977 interview with Cäcilia Rentmeister, which Schoppmann mentions, was cited by Marcella Schmidt in "Gertrude Sandmann (1893–1981)" in *Eldorado: Homosexuelle Frauen und Männer in Berlin 1850–1950*, ed. Berlin Museum, Berlin, 1992. See p. 206.

8 See Grau, report on a Luftwaffe assistant deported to a concentration camp in *Hidden Holocaust?* 82–83 and Schoppmann (*Nationalsozialistische Sexualpolitik und weibliche Homosexualität* (Frankfurt: Pfaffenweiler Presse, 1991, 232) for discussion of this specific case regarding the deportation of two female Luftwaffe assistants to concentration camps because one of them, Helen G., rejected the sexual advances of a male nazi lieutenant in the air signals corps where they both had worked, thus defying National Socialist conventions of war.

9 In addition, R. Klare, revising somewhat his earlier thesis in favor of criminalization, writes in "Die Homosexuellen als politisches Problem" (1938): "Female homosexuality should essentially be regarded as punishable behaviour, for it is likely to undermine blood values and to draw women away from their duties to the *Volk*. However, the special circumstances of the present time—above all, the great loss of men in the world war which has reduced women's prospects of marriage—do not make it seem appropriate that lesbianism should be prosecuted under the criminal law. The definition

of such an offence must be postponed because female homosexuality in its full extent is no longer simply substitute behaviour but an inner lack of stability" (R. Klare, "Die Homosexuellen als politisches Problem," Part Two: "Die weibliche Homosexualität" in *Der Hoheitsträger*, vol. 3, 1938, 17; qtd. in Grau, *Hidden Holocaust?* 84).

10 However, it need not be assumed that the domestic sphere is always already a signifier of heterosexuality alone as Gayatri Gopinath, in citing Geeta Patel, discusses in relation to Deepa Mehta's controversial 1996 film *Fire*, wherein female homosociality, as constituted by and constituting the domestic sphere, shifts into female desire, pleasure, and eroticism within the sanitized confines of the home, thereby destabilizing any causal, natural link between heterosexuality and the domestic (271). See also Geeta Patel, "Homely Housewives Run Amok: Lesbians in Marital Fixes" in *Public Culture* 16.1 (2004): 131–157.

11 For further discussion of this point, see Proctor, *Racial Hygiene*, chapter 5, titled "The Control of Women," especially for images of nazi propaganda (pp. 125ff.) on "The Decline of Marital Fecundity" (fig. 24) and causes in the declines of birth (fig. 26), which include, among other things, love of pleasure, women working outside the home, material comfort, and abortion.

12 Such loans ranged between 500 and 1000 RM, and by 1936 nazi officials had awarded over 500,000 loans valued at over 300 million RM (Friedman 15). After 1938, if a couple had been married for five years and had no child, they were penalized with a tax. See Proctor, *Racial Hygiene* 121. At the same time, anti-abortion laws were stringently enforced for Aryan women, except in cases where the mother's life was endangered. In addition, starting on Mother's Day in 1939, women were awarded the Honor Cross of German Motherhood (Ehrenkreuz den deutschen Mutter), awarded in bronze for four children, silver for six, and gold for eight (Proctor 120).

13 Nazi women's book, 1934, cited in Westenreider, *"Deutsche Frauen und Mädchen!"* 47.

14 Concerning prostitution, however, it is important to clarify that nazi views changed over time. Initially, women even suspected of being prostitutes or seeing a doctor for a sexually transmitted disease could be labelled as "loose women" and sent to a "work camp"; but state-regulated brothels were commonplace in the years leading up to the war and officially registered prostitutes were tolerated (see Gellately and Stoltzfus 12–13). The changed attitude was not incommensurate with nazi attitudes toward sex and pleasure not specifically tied to procreation, but rooted in sexual openness and experimentation strictly *within the confines of Aryan heterosexuality* as discussed earlier.

15 See Erica Fischer, *Aimée & Jaguar: A Love Story, Berlin 1943* (New York: HarperCollins, 1995), and the film that it inspired, *Aimée & Jaguar: Eine Liebe größer als der Tod*, dir. Max Färberböck, Zeitgeist Films, 1999.

16 See also Christa Schultz, "Weibliche Häftlinge aus Ravensbrück in Bordellen der Männerkonzentrationslager," *Frauen in Konzentrationslagern. Bergen-Belsen, Ravensbrück*, eds. Claus Füllberg-Stolberg et al., eds. (Bremen: Edition Temmen, 1994), 135–46.

17 For the specifics of the Luftwaffe assistant, see note 8 above.
18 This should give pause for reflection, given the several different versions of Anne Frank's *Diary* that have been published since the original, where Otto Frank edited out material considered to be too explicitly sexual. This is a point I will take up and discuss more fully in chapter 6.

4 Homosexuality and Fascism: A (Re)Analysis

1 From a postcolonial perspective on this point, see Spurlin, *Imperialism within the Margins: Queer Representation and the Politics of Culture in Southern Africa*, especially chapter 4. Certainly both European and postcolonial nationalisms might share this particular attribute (witness in France, for example, strategies of the Académie Française to prevent the anglicization of the French language, which is occurring through the influence of the English language mass media, electronic communication, and internet technology, and the 2004–05 controversy over Muslim schoolgirls not being allowed to wear veils in French public schools, which, along with other religious symbols, is seen to contradict the ideals of the secular French state). But European nationalism cannot be reduced to postcolonial nationalism or vice versa, since one must account for, as Partha Chatterjee notes, the difference of postcolonial nationalism(s) from the modular forms of national society propagated by the modern West (*Nation and Its Fragments* 5).
2 See Benedict Anderson, *Imagined Communities: Reflections on the Origin and Spread of Nationalism*.
3 The connection of male bonds to Enlightenment thinking is also worth noting, given the recognition of male friendships as an expression of virtue that served the general well being (I.S. Kon—see Oosterhuis 25, n35). Oosterhuis notes that the friendships could be not only emotional, but passionate and physical well into the middle of the nineteenth century, when such friendships began to be seen as threats to economic interests necessitating the confinement of emotion to the more traditional nuclear family, and when the friendships became subject to social surveillance with the increased medicalization of homosexuality later in the nineteenth century (Oosterhuis, "Homosexual Emancipation" 8–10). See also chapter 2 for further discussion of Adolf Brand and his friends who, in 1903, formed the *Gemeinschaft der Eigenen*, an ideological group that celebrated the love of male friends and was formed partly as an oppositional response to new meanings attached to male homosexuality by medical and psychiatric discourses at the time.
4 In their foreword to Theweleit's book, Jessica Benjamin and Anson Rabinbach compare fascist relations to authority with pre-oedipal relationships to primary identifications,

that is, to both a fear of and longing for a fusion against the threat of fragmentation and dissolution. In Lacanian terms, fascist males are "not yet fully born," that is, they have not fully entered the symbolic field of object relations that enables the differentiation of bodily boundaries. This, however, they note, should not be read as a desire to return to the primal unity with the mother, since the repudiation of the feminine is both a condition and effect of fascist homosocial bonding. See pp. xxi–xxii for further discussion.

5 Hewitt explains in his gloss of Adorno that the homosexual is a sadist only because he must perform the sadism of heterosexuality; thus, "his sadism is fueled by a frustration at the renunciation of primary masochistic desires" (*Political Inversions* 56).

6 Golsan and Hawthorne rely somewhat on David Carroll's argument (qtd. within the citation) in *French Literary Fascism*. See especially p. 148 in Carroll.

7 It would, of course, be simplistic to assume that fascism is simply the repression of homoerotic desire, given that nazi fascism incited desire both within the ranks of nazi power (Röhm), as well as among homosexuals in Germany, the occupied territories, and elsewhere. But this, I would argue, is part of a larger network of cultural meanings rather than simply being significant in and of itself. It would also be rather fallacious to conclude from this observation that nazi men were nothing more than repressed or latent homosexuals. A question that would then need to be asked, if one were to follow this line of pursuit, would be whether homosexuality is innately fascistic, which would be absurd in the absence of any analysis of historical or contextual contingencies. Such approaches, I would argue, override the cultural signification of homosexuality at a particular historical moment, in this case under National Socialism.

8 For further development of Lacan's theory of the constitution of the subject in/through language, see *Écrits: A Selection* and *The Seminars of Jacques Lacan (Books I–III)*.

9 Lacan is quite clear, however, that the imaginary and symbolic registers are neither simply oppositional nor purely sequential in that unconscious processes continue to put pressure on the symbolic (and on language) and interrupt its effective management. As Tamise van Pelt notes, even the adult desire to understand is a resistance to the "Oedipal injunction to difference," a denial of castration attendant upon entry into the symbolic, resulting in a fantasized sense of empowerment and agency (64).

10 One could argue for a more complete intersection of fascism and homosexuality if, for instance, fascists and homosexuals simply desire pleasure and intimacy with other males yet lack the object of desire; or, if men (whatever their sexuality), who are in high social positions with other men, desire unquestioned political power. But I am reluctant to concede to anything more than vague intersections, as these would have to vary according to particular personal, interpersonal, social, and historical contexts and an array of other contingencies. Foucault speaks of the ways in which sexuality is implicated in power but not in a simple hierarchical way. As I've noted earlier, he suggests that sexuality be thought of as "a great surface network in which the stimulation of

bodies, the intensification of pleasures, the incitement to discourse, the formation of special knowledges, the strengthening of controls and resistances, are linked to one another, in accordance with a few major strategies of knowledge and power" (105–6). The efficacy of maintaining a conflation of fascism with homosexuality, even among those who may occupy both of these subject positions, would collapse under the weight of the contingencies of the discursive network that would constitute the subjects in question and the objects of their desires.

11 I prefer to use the term "feminine" rather than the more clinically-grounded term "effeminate" to describe the internalization and embodiment of femininity in men, as it is simply more descriptive and less judgmental.

12 For further discussion, see my essay "Sissies and Sisters: Gender, Sexuality and the Possibilities of Coalition," especially p. 91.

13 Sartre insists, for example, that collaboration with the nazis was a feminine submission to the masculine order the nazis represented, supported by the fact of the numerous homosexuals in France who took part in nazi collaboration: "La collaborateur parle au nom de la force, mais il n'est pas la force.... Il me paraît qu'il y a là un curieux mélange de masochisme et de l'homosexualité" (Sartre 58; qtd. in Eribon 190–91). Sartre isn't only gendering collaborators as feminine, but bases his theory on the actual collaboration of homosexuals in France with the nazis. But his theory of collaboration falls apart somewhat if one were to consider homosexuals who participated in the resistance under nazi occupation and heterosexuals who were also collaborators.

14 Showing the different ways in which lesbians on the Left Bank of Paris in the 1920s and 1930s were politicized, Benstock notes that Djuna Barnes, Sylvia Beach, Hilda Doolittle (H.D.), and Janet Flanner took positions on the political left against totalitarian regimes that emerged in Europe after World War I (333).

5 Discursive Traces of Nazi Homophobia in Contemporary Culture

1 It was not until 1988 that the German Federal Republic first recognized the deportation of a single German homosexual. Further, Pierre Seel, a deported homosexual, was recognized in France as a victim of the nazis who did forced labor in an enemy-occupied, non-French territory between March 21, 1942, and September 26, 1942; was forced to serve in the German military from 1942 until 1945; and for his suffering and the dangers encountered, received a cheque for 9,100 francs (about $1,300) in the early 1990s from the French government (Seel 185n). But he was not recognized in any of the official documentation as a homosexual deportee.

2 The purging of lesbians and gay men from their military stations abroad was so intense after the war that thousands of lesbian and gay personnel were literally loaded on to "queer

ships" and sent to the nearest U.S. port on the East Coast (Boston, New York, Philadelphia, Baltimore, Miami) for those who had been stationed in Europe, or to the nearest U.S. port on the West Coast (Seattle, San Francisco, San Diego) for those stationed in Asia and the Pacific. As Lillian Faderman notes, many of those discharged believed they could not go home, and many stayed where they disembarked. This, in turn, helped to form large homosexual enclaves in port cities along both U.S. coasts (126).

3 The same tropes of national betrayal through homosexuality were redeployed in the later 1960s and early 1970s in the U.S. Black Power movement, where homosexuality practiced among black men was racialized in a different way from National Socialism, this time as a white aberration and as a betrayal of black nationalism. Interestingly, the Black Power movement also used the same tropes of failed gender borrowed from the homophobically-inscribed psychoanalytic research on homosexuality in the dominant white culture. For further discussion, see my essay "Culture, Rhetoric, and Queer Identity: James Baldwin and the Identity Politics of Race and Sexuality" in relation to the reception of the novels of African-American writer James Baldwin in the 1950s and early 1960s.

4 See Bieber et al., *Homosexuality: A Psychoanalytic Study*, which is a new edition of the 1962 publication reprinted in 1988 under the names of the original team of co-authors who were also the researchers in the 1952–62 study. In my citations to Bieber et al. I refer to the 1988 edition of the 1962 text (now out of print), which contains a new foreword by Irving and Toby Bieber in which they state that "the republication of this book deals with those same aspects [of the development of homosexuality, family dynamics, adaptive techniques, and the results of psychoanalytic therapy] exactly as written twenty-five years ago" (ix–x). The revised edition also acknowledges changed thinking on homosexuality since the time of its first publication, but is still largely a defense of the original findings. The foreword also claims that following the 1962 publication of the original research, follow-up work suggested that one-third of the homosexual patients had shifted to a heterosexual adaptation and that they remained exclusively heterosexual (i.e., "cured") in the intervening years (Bieber et al. xxiii).

5 It is important to note that the homosexual men in the H group in the Bieber study were a clinical population in the 1950s, which means that they were already undergoing psychological or psychiatric therapy either for their homosexuality or for other clinically diagnosed mental disorders. The difference between the two groups was not just with regard to sexual identity given that the heterosexual men in the control group were not in treatment at all and came from the general population. The comparative basis of the Bieber study was critiqued strongly by Evelyn Hooker, who in the late 1950s and early 1960s investigated non-patient homosexuals in the general population and found little significant differences in terms of their psychological health, social adjustment, ability to form long-lasting relationships, etc., as compared to heterosexuals. If there were difficulties in these areas, Hooker's data revealed that the major significant difference between the two groups was social hostility directed toward homosexuals in a largely heteronormative world. Hooker's work certainly played a role in changed

medical and psychiatric thinking on homosexuality later on. See Evelyn Hooker, "Male Homosexuals and Their 'Worlds'" in *Sexual Inversion*, ed. Judd Marmor (New York: Basic Books, 1965), p. 92, 95–98; and Evelyn Hooker, "The Adjustment of the Male Overt Homosexual" in *Journal of Projective Techniques* 21 (1957): 29–30.

6 For instance, in his *Three Essays on the Theory of Sexuality*, Freud remarks quite explicitly that inversion is explained "neither by the hypothesis that it is innate nor by the alternative hypothesis that it is acquired" (6). Bieber tried to de-link homosexuality from any sort of innateness in favor of an exclusively acquired and learned behavior unaffected by constitutional factors, which is contrary to Freudian thinking.

7 For further discussion of this point see Spurlin, "Sissies and Sisters: Gender, Sexuality and the Possibilities of Coalition."

8 In 1968, *DSM-II* appeared and noted homosexuality as psychopathological but no longer as a sociopathic disturbance. It was listed alongside other sexual "deviances," such as fetishism, pedophilia, transvestism, and exhibitionism.

9 The *DSM-III* retained "ego-dystonic homosexuality," reserved for those patients who were distressed by homosexual arousal and desired to acquire heterosexual arousal. The revised edition of the *DSM-III* (*DSM-III-R*), published in 1987, deleted ego-dystonic homosexuality as well. The current edition, *DSM-IV*, published in 1994, contains no entry for homosexuality.

10 See also Sandor Rado, "An Adaptational View of Sexual Behavior," in *Psychosexual Development in Health and Disease*, eds. Paul Hoch and Joseph Zubin (New York: Grune and Stratton, 1949); Edmund Bergler, "The Myth of a New National Disease: Homosexuality and the Kinsey Report," *Psychiatric Quarterly* 22.1 (1948): 66–88; Bergler's book *Homosexuality: Disease or Way of Life?* (New York: Hill and Wang, 1956); and Charles W. Socarides, *The Overt Homosexual* (New York: Grune and Stratton, 1968).

11 Earlier attempts at naming what we now know as AIDS were insufficient to describe it. Names such as GRID (Gay-Related Immune Deficiency) and AID (Acquired Immunodeficiency Disease) were given initially in response to the growing number of gay men in the United States with such opportunistic infections as Kaposi's sarcoma, a then-rare form of relatively benign cancer in the elderly, and *pneumocysitis carinni* pneumonia (PCP), a rare lung infection, both of which were nameable. Yet the overall cause for their occurrence in relatively young gay men was not. And there were still other contingencies, given that opportunistic infections began showing up in intravenous drug users, Haitians, and recipients of blood transfusions. On the history of names, see Altman's article in *The New York Times* (1982).

12 Speaking to this, Edelman gives an example of how the anti-homophobic slogan of ACT UP, Silence = Death, was reappropriated into an ideology of homophobia in the form of graffiti inscribed on a wall at New York University, which said "Gay Rights = AIDS." Both Silence = Death and its homophobic counterpart are discursive events that clarify how different groups see AIDS as threatening the social structures through which they have constituted their identities (Edelman 296–97). This also reveals how

136 | *Notes*

language can never simply reflect the material world or the conscious intentions of its speaker, but is always already a social invention whose meaning cannot be controlled and held completely determinate within the public sphere of social deliberation.

13 Protease inhibitors (PIs) first appeared in 1995 and block the protease enzyme that HIV needs in order to replicate itself once it infects a human cell. Protease inhibitors reduce the amount of virus in the blood and increase CD 4 cell counts even if they are already very low.

14 Anti-retroviral drug therapy builds on the work of protease inhibitors mentioned above and consists of combinations of drugs to slow down further the replication of HIV in the body. The drugs are taken in combination (usually three or more) so that in case a new strain of HIV is produced and is resistant to one type of drug (such as protease inhibitors), it would not be able to replicate itself quickly. Taking three or more anti-retroviral drugs at the same time reduces significantly the rate at which viral resistance would develop. Combinations usually consist of two nucleoside/nucleotide reverse transcriptase inhibitors (NRTIs) combined with either a non-nucleoside reverse transcriptase inhibitor (NNRTI) or a boosted protease inhibitor.

15 It must also be noted that despite the deployment of the powerful discourses of medicine, health care, and government authority, global and local activism in South Africa has blatantly resisted international drug policies and rationales for distribution practices. The Treatment Action Campaign (TAC) in South Africa fought successfully against international pharmaceutical companies who were profiting largely at the expense of those who suffered from HIV/AIDS in the poorer nations of the world. The TAC willfully ignored international trade agreements that prohibited, at the time, the import of less costly generic versions of the three separately patented anti-retroviral drugs and the combination of these generic versions into a single medication for the treatment of HIV infection. At the same time, TAC also exposed the bureaucratic inefficiency of the South African government under Mbeki to manage the HIV/AIDS crisis effectively. Similarly, the French non-governmental human rights organization *Médecins sans Frontières* has worked in impoverished townships in South Africa by importing generic versions of anti-retroviral drugs from Brazil and defying globalized assumptions that hold that poor Africans are too uneducated and irresponsible to follow the strict regimen of doses required. For further discussion see Spurlin, *Imperialism within the Margins*, especially pp. 126–27.

16 See Spurlin, *Imperialism within the Margins*, for a more detailed discussion of this point, especially pp. 94–96.

6 Queer Sexuality, Holocaust Studies, and the Challenge of Democratic Futurity

1 Evans also discusses how racial hygiene became an academic discipline under the Weimar Republic with the founding of the first chair in the subject at Munich University in

1923 and the development of forty or more courses in racial hygiene and related areas of study over the next nine years at German universities in general (33).
2. Though it is important to point out that work on homosexuality did begin to take shape in the 1980s largely in the form of survivor testimony. See chapter 1.
3. Rosenfeld wonders "how any story of the crimes of the Nazi era can remain faithful to the specific features of those events and at the same time address contemporary American social and political agendas" (qtd. in Flanzbaum 5; see Alvin Rosenfeld, "The Americanization of the Holocaust," *Commentary* [June 1995]: 35).
4. See Michael Warner, *Publics and Counterpublics* (New York: Zone Books, 2005), p. 89.
5. Edelman is quite clear that he is not referring to the lived experiences of particular children, but to the iconic image of the Child (*No Future* 11) as symbolic of the reproduction and perpetuation of the social order.
6. See Spurlin, *Imperialism within the Margins*, chapter 5, especially pp. 119–20, and Patton, *Globalizing AIDS*, especially chapter 3. While anti-retroviral drugs have been distributed through government clinics in South Africa since 2004 (though far from reaching the majority of those who are HIV infected), Mbeki still questions the scientific link between HIV and AIDS and sees safer-sex programs and anti-AIDS campaigns in South Africa as forms of a western conspiracy to control African sexuality.
7. Though again, as I mentioned in the previous note, anti-retroviral drugs issued through the national health care system in South Africa are still not reaching all of those who need them.
8. Speaking to this from a somewhat similar point of view, José Esteban Muñoz reminds us that Edelman's reproductive thesis, to the extent that it depends on a questioning of social community and social belonging, runs the risk of deferring other differences in relation to sexuality, such as race and gender, which has traditionally been the privilege of western, white, gay male scholars (825–26).
9. Prior to the Final Solution came a series of racial legislative measures tied to the protection and perpetuation of Aryan citizenry, all of which were attached to a regime of intense reproductive futurity through the protection of the purity of German blood for future generations. For example, the Civil Service Law of 1933 (Gesetz zur Wiederherstellung des Berufsbeamtentums) required proof of Aryan ancestry to hold government jobs; the Blood Protection Law of September 1935 (Gesetz zum Schutze des deutschen Blutes und der deutschen Ehre) prohibited marriage or sexual relations between Jews and Germans; and the Marital Health Law in October of the same year (Gesetz zum Schutze der Erbgesundheit des deutschen Volkes) required a certificate of health for a marriage license. For further discussion on German racial legislation and the establishment of genetic health courts under National Socialism, see Proctor, *Racial Hygiene* 101–4.
10. However, Heineman does acknowledge that in Holocaust studies courses, sexuality, as a vector of nazi power, is often "bracketed off" as women's or as gay history (65) if the topic is about controlling reproduction and women's bodies or about the persecution of gay men respectively.

11 Alexander here is specifically discussing the U.S. justification of its deployment of troops to Iraq under President George Herbert Walker Bush in 1990 following Iraq's invasion of Kuwait and the justification of Operation Desert Storm when the actual fighting began in 1991. But the same tropes of the cultural legitimation of hate and the gendering of western white masculinity, and the feminization of oriental masculinity, would apply similarly in a heightened, intensified sense, to the U.S.-led mission against Iraq in 2003 given the precedence of 9/11, whereby many in the administration of George W. Bush linked Saddam Hussein with al-Qaeda as a means to justify the multinational coalition and, at the same time, mislead the public.

References

Adorno, Theodor. *Minima Moralia: Reflections from a Damaged Life*. 1951. Trans. E.F.N. Jephcott. London: Verso, 1951.
Ahmed, Sara. *Queer Phenomenology: Orientations, Objects, Others*. Durham: Duke University Press, 2006.
"Aids Orphans' Survival Offers Africa Hope." *Observer*. May 25, 2003: 5.
Alexander, M. Jacqui. "Erotic Autonomy as a Politics of Decolonization: An Anatomy of Feminist and State Practice in the Bahamas Tourist Economy." *Feminist Genealogies, Colonial Legacies, Democratic Futures*. Eds. M. Jacqui Alexander and Chandra Talpade Mohanty. New York: Routledge, 1997. 63–100.
———. *Pedagogies of Crossing: Meditations on Feminism, Sexual Politics, Memory, and the Sacred*. Durham: Duke University Press, 2005.
Altman, L.K. "New Homosexual Disorder Worries Officials." *The New York Times*. May 11, 1982.
Amnesty International. *Crimes of Hate, Conspiracy of Silence: Torture and Ill-Treatment Based on Sexual Identity*. London: Amnesty International Publications, 2001.
Anderson, Benedict. *Imagined Communities: Reflections on the Origin and Spread of Nationalism*. London: Verso, 1983.
Arendt, Hannah. *The Origins of Totalitarianism*. New York: Harcourt, 1968.
Bartov, Omer. "Antisemitism, the Holocaust, and Reinterpretations of National Socialism." Berenbaum and Peck. 75–98.
Bayer, Ronald. *Homosexuality and American Psychiatry: The Politics of Diagnosis*. 1981. Princeton: Princeton University Press, 1987.
Beck, Gad. *An Underground Life: Memoirs of a Gay Jew in Nazi Berlin*. Trans. Allison Brown. Madison: University of Wisconsin Press, 1999.
Benjamin, Jessica, and Anson Rabinbach. "Foreword." Theweleit. ix–xxv.

Benstock, Shari. "Paris Lesbianism and the Politics of Reaction, 1900–1940." *Hidden from History: Reclaiming the Gay and Lesbian Past*. Eds. Martin Duberman, Martha Vicinus, and George Chauncey, Jr. New York: Meridian, 1990. 332–46.

Berenbaum, Michael. "The Uniqueness and Universality of the Holocaust." Berenbaum. *Mosaic of Victims*. 20–36.

———, ed. *A Mosaic of Victims: Non-Jews Persecuted and Murdered by the Nazis*. New York: New York University Press, 1990.

———, and Abraham J. Peck, eds. *The Holocaust and History: The Known, the Unknown, the Disputed, and the Reexamined*. Bloomington: Indiana University Press, 1998.

Bersani, Leo. *Homos*. Cambridge: Harvard University Press, 1995.

Bieber, Irving, et al. *Homosexuality: A Psychoanalytic Study*. Northvale, NJ: Aronson, 1988.

Bowie, Malcolm. *Lacan*. Cambridge: Harvard University Press, 1991.

Brenkman, John. *Straight Male Modern: A Cultural Critique of Psychoanalysis*. New York: Routledge, 1993.

Bunzl, Matti. *Symptoms of Modernity: Jews and Queers in Late-Twentieth-Century Vienna*. Berkeley: University of California Press, 2004.

Bush, Barbara. *Imperialism, Race and Resistance: Africa and Britain, 1919–1945*. London: Routledge, 1999.

Butler, Judith. *Bodies That Matter: On the Discursive Limits of "Sex."* New York: Routledge, 1993.

———. *Gender Trouble: Feminism and the Subversion of Identity*. 1990. New York: Routledge, 1999.

Carroll, David. *French Literary Fascism: Nationalism, Anti-Semitism, and the Ideology of Culture*. Princeton: Princeton University Press, 1995.

Chari, Hema. "Colonial Fantasies and Postcolonial Identities: Elaboration of Postcolonial Masculinity and Homoerotic Desire." *Postcolonial, Queer: Theoretical Intersections*. Ed. John C. Hawley. Albany: State University of New York Press, 2001. 277–304.

Chatterjee, Partha. *The Nation and Its Fragments: Colonial and Postcolonial Histories*. Princeton: Princeton University Press, 1993.

———. *Nationalist Thought and the Colonial World: A Derivative Discourse*. 1986. Minneapolis: University of Minnesota Press, 2001.

Corber, Robert J. *Homosexuality in Cold War America: Resistance and the Crisis of Masculinity*. Durham: Duke University Press, 1997.

Derrida, Jacques. *Of Grammatology*. 1967. Trans. Gayatri Chakravorty Spivak. Baltimore: Johns Hopkins University Press, 1976.

De Saussure, Ferdinand. *Course in General Linguistics*. 1916. Eds. Charles Bally, Albert Sechehaye, and Albert Reidlinger. Trans. Wade Baskin. London: Fontana, 1974.

Diagnostic and Statistical Manual of Mental Disorders. 4th ed. Washington, DC: American Psychiatric Association, 1994.

Eberhard, Ehrhard F.W. *Die Frauenbewegung und irhe erotischen Grundlagen.* Vienna: Braumueller, 1924.
Edelman, Lee. *No Future: Queer Theory and the Death Drive.* Durham: Duke University Press, 2004.
———. "The Plague of Discourse: Politics, Literary Theory, and AIDS." *Displacing Homophobia: Gay Male Perspectives in Literature and Culture.* Eds. Ronald R. Butters, John M. Clum, and Michael Moon. Durham: Duke University Press, 1989. 289–305.
Elman, R. Amy. "Lesbians and the Holocaust." Fuchs. 9–17.
Epprecht, Marc. *Hungochani: The History of a Dissident Sexuality in Southern Africa.* Montreal and Kingston: McGill-Queen's University Press, 2004.
Eribon, Didier. *Hérésies: Essais sur la théorie de la sexualité.* Paris: Fayard, 2003.
Evans, Richard J. "Social Outsiders in German History: From the Sixteenth Century to 1933." Gellately and Stoltzfus. *Social Outsiders in Nazi Germany.* 20–44.
Eze, Emmanuel Chukwudi. "Beyond Dichotomies: Communicative Action and Cultural Hegemony." *Beyond Dichotomies: Histories, Identities, Cultures, and the Challenge of Globalization.* Ed. Elisabeth Mudimbe-Boyi. Albany: State University of New York Press, 2002. 49–68.
Faderman, Lillian. *Odd Girls and Twilight Lovers: A History of Lesbian Life in Twentieth-Century America.* New York: Penguin, 1991.
Farwell, Marilyn R. "Heterosexual Plots and Lesbian Subtexts: Toward a Theory of Lesbian Narrative Space." Jay and Glasgow. 91–103.
Feig, Konnilyn. "Non-Jewish Victims in the Concentration Camps." Berenbaum. *Mosaic of Victims.* 161–78.
"Fighting Back. Special Report: AIDS in Southern Africa." *The Economist.* May 11, 2002. 27–29.
Flanzbaum, Hilene, ed. *The Americanization of the Holocaust.* Baltimore: The Johns Hopkins University Press, 1999.
Foucault, Michel. *The History of Sexuality. Volume 1: An Introduction.* Trans. Robert Hurley. 1978. New York: Vintage, 1980.
Frank, Anne. *Anne Frank: The Diary of a Young Girl.* 1947. New York: Pocket Books, 1958.
Freud, Sigmund. *Three Essays on the Theory of Sexuality.* Trans. James Strachey. New York: Basic Books, 1962.
Friedman, Jonathan C. *Speaking the Unspeakable: Essays on Sexuality, Gender, and Holocaust Survivor Memory.* Lanham, MD: University Press of America, 2002.
Friedman, Richard C. *Male Homosexuality: A Contemporary Psychoanalytic Perspective.* New Haven: Yale University Press, 1988.
Fuchs, Esther, ed. *Women and the Holocaust: Narrative and Representation.* Lanham, MD: University Press of America, 1999.

Gellately, Robert, and Nathan Stoltzfus. "Social Outsiders and the Construction of the Community of the People." Gellately and Stoltzfus. *Social Outsiders in Nazi Germany*. 3–19.

———, eds. *Social Outsiders in Nazi Germany*. Princeton: Princeton University Press, 2001.

Giles, Geoffrey J. "The Denial of Homosexuality: Same-Sex Incidents in Himmler's SS and Police." *Journal of the History of Sexuality* 11.1–2 (2002): 256–90.

———. "The Institutionalization of Homosexual Panic in the Third Reich." Gellately and Stoltzfus. *Social Outsiders in Nazi Germany*. 233–55.

Gilman, Sander L. *Difference and Pathology: Stereotypes of Sexuality, Race, and Madness*. Ithaca: Cornell University Press, 1985.

Gopinath, Gayatri. "Nostalgia, Desire, Diaspora: South Asian Sexualities in Motion." *Theorizing Diaspora*. Eds. Jana Evans Braziel and Anita Mannur. Malden, MA: Blackwell Publishing, 2003. 261–79.

Grau, Günter. "Final Solution of the Homosexual Question? The Antihomosexual Policies of the Nazis and the Social Consequences for Homosexual Men." Berenbaum and Peck. 338–44.

———, ed. *Hidden Holocaust? Gay and Lesbian Persecution in Germany 1933–45*. 1993. Trans. Patrick Camiller. London: Cassell, 1995.

Gregor, Neil, Nils Roemer, and Mark Roseman, eds. *German History from the Margins*. Bloomington: Indiana University Press, 2006.

Halperin, David M. *How To Do the History of Homosexuality*. Chicago: University of Chicago Press, 2002.

Harper, Phillip Brian. "Gay Male Identities, Personal Privacy, and Relations of Public Exchange: Notes on Directions for Queer Critique." *Social Text* 15.3–4 (1997): 5–29.

Hauser, Gerard A. "Rhetorical Democracy and Civic Engagement." *Rhetorical Democracy: Discursive Practices of Civic Engagement*. Eds. Gerard A. Hauser and Amy Grim. Mahwah, NJ: Lawrence Erlbaum Publishers, 2004. 1–14.

Hawthorne, Melanie. "(En)Gendering Fascism: Rachilde's 'Les Vendanges de Sodome' and *Les Hors-Nature*." Hawthorne and Golsan. 27–48.

———, and Richard J. Golsan, eds. *Gender and Fascism in Modern France*. Hanover, NH: University Press of New England, 1997.

Heger, Heinz. *The Men with the Pink Triangle: The True Life-and-Death Story of Homosexuals in the Nazi Death Camps*. 1980. Trans. David Fernbach. Boston: Alyson, 1994.

Heineman, Elizabeth D. "Sexuality and Nazism: The Double Unspeakable?" 2002. *Sexuality and German Fascism*. Ed. Dagmar Herzog. New York: Berghahn Books, 2005. 22–66.

Herzog, Dagmar. "Hubris and Hypocrisy, Incitement and Disavowal: Sexuality and German Fascism." *Journal of the History of Sexuality* 11.1–2 (2002): 3–21.

———. *Sex after Fascism: Memory and Morality in Twentieth-Century Germany*. Princeton: Princeton University Press, 2005.

Hewitt, Andrew. *Political Inversions: Homosexuality, Fascism, and the Modernist Imaginary.* Stanford: Stanford University Press, 1996.

———. "Sleeping with the Enemy: Genet and the Fantasy of Homo-Fascism." Hawthorne and Golsan. 119–40.

Hirsch, Marianne, and Irene Kacandes, eds. *Teaching the Representation of the Holocaust.* New York: Modern Language Association of America, 2004.

Hirschfeld, Magnus. "Die objektive Diagnose der Homosexualität." *Jahrbuch für sexuelle Zwischenstufen* 1 (1899): 4–35.

"Homosexuality in America." *Life.* June 26, 1964: 66–80.

"Homosexuals: Victims of the Nazi Era." Report of the United States Holocaust Memorial Museum. http://www.holocaust-trc.org/homosx.htm.

Horowitz, Sara R. "Gender and Holocaust Representation." Hirsch and Kacandes. 110–22.

Jay, Karla, and Joanne Glasgow, eds. *Lesbian Texts and Contexts: Radical Revisions.* New York: New York University Press, 1990.

Kinsey, Alfred, et al. *Sexual Behavior in the Human Male.* Philadelphia: Saunders, 1948.

Kon, I.S. *Freundschaft, Geschichte und Sozialpsychologie der Freundschaft als soziale Institution und individuelle Beziehung.* Hamburg: Rowohlt Verlag, 1979.

Lacan, Jacques. *Écrits: A Selection.* 1966. Trans. Alan Sheridan. New York: W.W. Norton, 1977.

———. *The Seminar of Jacques Lacan. Book I: Freud's Papers on Technique 1953–1954.* Trans. John Forrester. Ed. Jacques-Alain Miller. New York: W.W. Norton, 1991.

———. *The Seminar of Jacques Lacan. Book II: The Ego in Freud's Theory and in the Technique of Psychoanalysis 1954–1955.* Trans. Sylvana Tomaselli. Ed. Jacques-Alain Miller. New York: W.W. Norton, 1988.

———. *The Seminar of Jacques Lacan. Book III: The Psychoses 1955–1956.* Trans. Russell Grigg. Ed. Jacques-Alain Miller. New York: W.W. Norton, 1993.

Lautmann, Rüdiger. "The Pink Triangle: Homosexuals as 'Enemies of the State'." Berenbaum and Peck. 345–57.

Lyotard, Jean-François. *The Differend: Phrases in Dispute.* 1983. Trans. Georges Van Den Abbeele. Minneapolis: University of Minnesota Press, 1988.

Marrus, Michael R. "The Holocaust: Where We Are, Where We Need to Go—A Comment." Berenbaum and Peck. 30–34.

McClintock, Anne. *Imperial Leather: Race, Gender and Sexuality in the Colonial Contest.* New York: Routledge, 1995.

Micheler, Stefan. "Homophobic Propaganda and the Denunciation of Same-Sex Desiring Men under National Socialism." *Journal of the History of Sexuality* 11.1–2 (2002): 95–130.

Milton, Sybil H. "'Gypsies' as Social Outsiders in Nazi Germany." Gellately and Stoltzfus. *Social Outsiders in Nazi Germany.* 212–32.

Mosse, George L. *The Fascist Revolution: Toward a General Theory of Fascism.* New York: Howard Fertig, 1999.

Mosse, George L. *Nationalism and Sexuality: Respectability and Abnormal Sexuality in Modern Europe.* New York: Howard Fertig, 1985.

Muñoz, José Esteban. "Thinking Beyond Antirelationality and Antiutopianism in Queer Critique." *PMLA* 121.3 (2006): 825–26.

Oosterhuis, Harry. "Homosexual Emancipation in Germany Before 1933: Two Traditions." Oosterhuis and Kennedy. 1–27.

———. "Introduction: Political Issues and the Rise of Nazism." Oosterhuis and Kennedy. 183–92.

———. "Male Bonding and Homosexuality in German Nationalism." Oosterhuis and Kennedy. 241–63.

———, and Hubert Kennedy, eds. *Homosexuality and Male Bonding in Pre-Nazi Germany: The Youth Movement, the Gay Movement, and Male Bonding Before Hitler's Rise.* Trans. Hubert Kennedy. London: Haworth Press, 1991.

Patton, Cindy. *Globalizing AIDS.* Minneapolis: University of Minnesota Press, 2002.

———. *Inventing AIDS.* New York: Routledge, 1990.

Plant, Richard. *The Pink Triangle: The Nazi War Against Homosexuals.* New York: Henry Holt, 1986.

Proctor, Robert N. *Racial Hygiene: Medicine under the Nazis.* Cambridge: Harvard University Press, 1988.

Rich, Adrienne. "Compulsory Heterosexuality and Lesbian Existence." 1980. *Blood, Bread, and Poetry: Selected Prose 1979–1985.* New York: W.W. Norton, 1986. 23–75.

Ringelheim, Joan Miriam. "The Unethical and the Unspeakable: Women and the Holocaust." *Simon Wiesenthal Annual* 1 (1984): 69–87.

Rittner, Carol. "The Triumph of Memory." Foreword. Berenbaum. *Mosaic of Victims.* xi–xv.

Roellig, Ruth Margarete. *Berlins lesbische Frauen/Les Lesbiennes de Berlin.* 1928. Bilingual ed. Trans. Charles Adam. *Cahiers Gay-Kitsch-Camp* 16. 1992.

Röll, Wolfgang. "Homosexual Inmates in the Buchenwald Concentration Camp." *Journal of Homosexuality* 31.4 (1996): 1–28.

Said, Edward. *Orientalism.* New York: Vintage, 1979.

Sartre, Jean-Paul. "Qu'est-ce qu'un collaborateur?" *Situation III.* Paris: Gallimard, 1949. 43–61.

Schoppmann, Claudia. "The Campaign Against Homosexuality and Its Effects on Lesbians." Unpublished paper. Conference on the Persecution of Homosexuals under the Nazi Regime. United States Holocaust Memorial Museum. Washington, DC. 2000.

———. *Days of Masquerade: Life Stories of Lesbians During the Third Reich.* 1993. Trans. Allison Brown. New York: Columbia University Press, 1996.

———. "The Position of Lesbian Women in the Nazi Period." Grau. *Hidden Holocaust?* 8–15.

Sedgwick, Eve Kosofsky. "How To Bring Your Kids Up Gay: The War on Effeminate Boys." 1991. *Tendencies.* Durham: Duke University Press, 1993. 154–64.

———. "Privilege of Unknowing: Diderot's *The Nun*." 1988. *Tendencies*. Durham: Duke University Press, 1993. 23–51.
Seel, Pierre. *Liberation Was for Others: Memoirs of a Gay Survivor of the Nazi Holocaust*. 1994. Trans. Joachim Neugroschel. New York: Da Capo Press, 1997.
Sontag, Susan. *AIDS and Its Metaphors*. New York: Farrar, Straus and Giroux, 1989.
Spivak, Gayatri Chakravorty. *A Critique of Postcolonial Reason: Toward a History of the Vanishing Present*. Cambridge: Harvard University Press, 1999.
Spurlin, William J. "Culture, Rhetoric, and Queer Identity: James Baldwin and the Identity Politics of Race and Sexuality." *James Baldwin Now*. Ed. Dwight A. McBride. New York: New York University Press, 1999. 103–21.
———. *Imperialism within the Margins: Queer Representation and the Politics of Culture in Southern Africa*. New York: Palgrave-USA, 2006.
———. "Sissies and Sisters: Gender, Sexuality and the Possibilities of Coalition." *Coming Out of Feminism?* Eds. Mandy Merck, Naomi Segal, and Elizabeth Wright. Oxford: Blackwell Publishers, 1998. 74–101.
Stimpson, Catharine R. "Lesbian Studies in the 1990s." Jay and Glasgow. 377–82.
Sullivan, Andrew. *Virtually Normal: An Argument about Homosexuality*. New York: Vintage, 1996.
———. "When Plagues End: Notes on the Twilight of an Epidemic." *The New York Times Magazine*. November 10, 1996: 52–62.
Theweleit, Klaus. *Male Fantasies, Volume 2. Male Bodies: Psychoanalyzing the White Terror*. 1978. Trans. Erica Carter and Chris Turner. Minneapolis: University of Minnesota Press, 1989.
Van Dijk, Lutz, ed. *La déportation des homosexuels. Onze témoignages: Allemagne 1933–1945*. Trans. Charles Adam. Montblanc: H & O Editions, 2000.
Vanita, Ruth, ed. *Queering India: Same-Sex Love and Eroticism in Indian Culture and Society*. New York: Routledge, 2002.
Van Pelt, Tamise. *The Other Side of Desire: Lacan's Theory of the Registers*. Albany: State University of New York Press, 2000.
Westenrieder, Norbert. *"Deutsche Frauen und Mädchen!" vom Alltagsleben 1933–1945*. Düsseldorf: Droste, 1984.
World Health Organization. "Towards Universal Access: Sealing Up Priority HIV/AIDS Interventions in the Public Sector." April 17, 2007.
Wright, Elizabeth. *Psychoanalytic Criticism: A Reappraisal*. 2nd ed. Cambridge: Polity Press, 1998.
Zahn, Gordon C. "Pacifists during the Third Reich." Berenbaum. *Mosaic of Victims*. 194–99.
Zucker, Kenneth, and Susan Bradley. *Gender Identity Disorder and Psychosexual Problems in Children and Adolescents*. New York: Guilford Press, 1995.

Index

ACT UP (AIDS Coalition to Unleash Power) 97
Adorno, Theodor 11, 69, 71
Africa 23
   cultural nationalism 101–2
   HIV/AIDS crisis in 98–105
   peripherization of 99, 116
Afrikaners 6–7
Ahmed, Sara 112–13
AIDS, *see* HIV/AIDS crisis
Aimee & Jaguar (Fischer) 60
Alexander, M. Jacqui 116, 118, 119, 138n11
Allied Military Government 88
American Psychiatric Association (APA) 86, 90, 92
Anderson, Benedict 66
Anglo-Boer War 23
anti-retroviral drugs 100–1, 118, 136n14, 137n7
anti-Semitism 8, 16, 22, 31, 34, 44, 82, 110
apartheid 6–7, 22–4, 115
Arab/Islamic masculinity 119, 138n11
Arendt, Hannah 9, 22, 23

Aryan racial purity 17, 20, 109–10
asocials 57, 63
Austria 56–7, 86

Barney, Natalie 82
Bartov, Omar 4, 110
Bayer, Ronald 90–1, 93
Benstock, Shari 82, 133n14
Berenbaum, Michael 16, 17
Berlin's Lesbian Women (Roellig) 48
Bersani, Leo 80, 114
bestiality 45
Bieber, Irving 12, 90, 91, 92, 134n5
Black Power movement 134n3
Bowie, Malcolm 29
Bradley, Susan 92
Brenkman, John 79, 80
British imperialism 23
Brookes, Romaine 82
Bush, Barbara 7, 23
Butler, Judith 32, 42, 46, 77

castration 75, 76–7, 80
Catholic Church 38

Center for Advanced Holocaust Studies 2
Central Reich Office for Combating Homosexuality and Abortion 9, 32, 34–6, 125n10, 126n11
Chari, Hema 69–70
Chatterjee, Partha 25, 66
Chauncey, George A. 82
childhood effeminacy 86, 90, 91–4, 104, 107
Cloister Trials 38
Cold War 88, 91, 93
colonialism 22–5, 116, 118–19
communism 11–12, 73, 82
comradeship 39–41, 67–8, 127n19
concentration camps 43–4, 60–1, 88, 128n20
Corber, Robert J. 88, 89
cultural stereotypes 89

decolonization 23, 25, 85
degeneracy 6, 17, 31, 33, 37, 42–3
Derrida, Jacques 75–6
Diagnostic and Statistical Manual of Mental Disorders 12, 86, 90–1, 91–2, 93, 94, 104, 122n3
Diary of Anne Frank, The 111–13, 131n18
différend 96, 97, 104
domestic sphere 10–11, 41–2, 47, 54–5, 63, 107, 130n10

Eberhard, Ehrhard F.W. 49, 53, 129n6
Edelman, Lee 97, 114, 115, 116, 135n12, 137n5
ego-dystonic homosexuality 135n9
Elman, R. Amy 52, 53, 54, 57, 59–60, 61–2
Enlightenment 76, 131n3
Eribon, Didier 81–2, 133n13
erotic autonomy 10, 13, 38, 40, 45, 50, 51, 56, 86, 106, 116, 119–20

eugenics 7–8, 33, 43, 109
Evans, Richard 33, 109, 136n1
Eze, Emmanuel 99

Faderman, Lillian 51
Falwell, Jerry 95
Farwell, Marilyn 51, 60
fascism; *see also* nazism
    homosexuality and 5, 11–12, 65–84, 132n7, 132n10
    imperialism and 22–4
    masculinity and 67–71
fellatio 76–8
femininity 32, 41–2, 56
    repudiation of 11, 69, 70, 80
feminization
    fear of 27
    of gay men 33, 34, 42
    of Jews 33, 34, 42, 43
Final Solution 34, 44, 47, 109, 110
Fischer, Erica 60
Flanzbaum, Hilene 111, 112
Foucault, Michel 18–21, 36, 37, 74–5, 132–3n10
France 68, 81, 82, 133n13
Frank, Anne 61–2, 111–12, 131n18
Frankfurt School 11, 73
Freikorps 11, 79, 83
Freud, Sigmund 74, 90, 135n6
Freundesliebe 39
Friedman, Jonathan 43–4, 46–7, 55, 130n12
Friedman, Richard 92
Fuchs, Esther 46, 47

gay men, *see* homosexuals
Gemeinschaft der Eigenen 39–41, 41–2, 67, 131n3
gender atypical boys 92–3

Gender Identity Disorder in Childhood
  (GIDC) 86, 91–4, 104, 107
German Federal Republic 86–8, 133n1
German nationalism 8–9, 17, 20, 41,
  124n11
Gestapo 34, 35
Giles, Geoffrey 34, 35, 36, 37, 41, 42, 43
Global Programme on AIDS 102–3
Golsan, Richard 71
Grau, Günter 5, 30–1, 35–6, 43, 44,
  87–8, 110, 125n4
Great Trek 7

Halperin, David 18, 20, 21
Harper, Phillip Brian 19, 98
Hauser, Gerard 118
Hawthorne, Melanie 79, 81
Heger, Heinz 87
Heineman, Elizabeth 4, 118, 137n10
Helms Amendment 95
Herzog, Dagmar 5–6, 30, 31, 38, 86,
  119, 123n8
Hewitt, Andrew 11, 34, 37, 69, 72, 73,
  75, 76–7, 78, 132n5
Himmler, Heinrich 9, 31, 32, 34, 35, 43,
  125n6, 125n9, 126n11
Hirschfeld, Magnus 38, 40, 48–9, 128n3,
  129n4
HIV/AIDS crisis 12–13, 85, 94–105,
  107, 115, 118, 119
Holocaust
  gender politics and 2–4
  Judaic significance of 15–16
  narratives of sexuality and 4–5
  purity of 111
  significance of 111–13
  uniqueness of 13, 109–10
Holocaust scholarship 8–9, 13–14
  comparisons in 109–10
  future of 110–20

Jewish/non-Jewish split 15–17
lesbian status and 60–3
marginalization of homosexuality
  in 110–11, 117
masculine bias in 3–4, 47–8, 80
queer studies within 15–27
Holocaust victims
  differentiation of 29
  homosexual 9, 15, 29–30, 122n4
  Jewish/non-Jewish split 15–16
  Jews 15–16, 109–10
  lesbian 56–8, 60–1
  reparations for 86–7
homo-fascism 73–4
homosexuality
  criminalization of 9, 12, 18, 30–1, 37,
    45, 71, 85–6, 117, 119, 121n3,
    123n5
  ego-dystonic 135n9
  etiology of 36, 43, 90
  fascism and 5, 11–12, 65–84, 132n7,
    132n10
  as foreign to indigenous culture 26,
    102–3
  latent 11, 18, 69, 71–4, 76, 83,
    128n20, 132n7
  marginalization of, in Holocaust
    studies 110–11, 117
  medical pathologization of 20, 89, 90–1
  nazi juridical discourse and 29–44
Hooker, Evelyn 134n5
Horowitz, Sara 17–18, 48
Hussein, Saddam 119, 138n11
hypermasculinity 5, 11, 42, 69–71, 80,
  128n20
hysteria 9, 33, 42

imperialism 9, 22–5, 26, 27, 99, 102,
  118, 119, 124n9
India 23

indigenous cultures 25–6, 85, 102–3, 116, 121n3
Islamic law 105–6

Jews
  effeminization of 33, 34, 42, 73
  portrayals of 33, 34
  sexuality of 32, 38
  women 46–7
  as victims in Holocaust 15–17, 109–10

Kinsey Report 12, 88–9, 90
Klare, Rudolf 53

Lacan, Jacques 76, 77, 79, 132n8, 132n9
latent homosexuality 11, 18, 69, 71–4, 76, 83, 128n20, 132n7
Lautmann, Rüdiger 87
lesbians 10–11, 45–63
  avant-garde 82–3
  contemporary homophobia and 106–7
  criminalization of 52–3, 56–7, 116, 129n9
  enforced conformity by 58–60
  invisibility of 51–2, 56
  life stories of 49–51
  persecution of, under nazis 17–18, 45–6, 53–4, 56–8
  sent to concentration camps 58–9, 60–1, 129n8
  subculture 48–50, 51
linguistic signification 75–6, 77
Lyotardian *différend* 96, 97, 104

male friendship 39–41, 67, 68, 131n3
male homosociality 39, 67–72, 75, 89, 127n19
Mandela, Winnie 121n3
Männerbund 11, 39, 40–2, 67, 68

Marrus, Michael R. 117
masculinity 32, 40–3, 79, 80
  Arab/Islamic 119, 138n11
  fascism and 67–71
  hypermasculinity 5, 11, 42, 69–71, 80, 128n20
masculinization in women 55
Mbeki, Thabo 101, 115, 136n15
McClintock, Anne 7, 102
medical discourses 33, 33–4, 37, 39–40, 42, 90–105
Micheler, Stefan 32, 35, 36, 59, 125n7, 126n13
Milton, Sybil H. 109
Mosse, George 31, 32, 33–4, 37, 38, 41, 65, 67, 68, 125n9, 126n14, 127n18
motherhood 32, 46, 55, 56, 90, 130n12
Müller, Johann Valentin 126n14

National Socialism 11;
  see also nazism; Third Reich
  inferior races 23, 33–4, 38, 46, 57
  juridical practices under 30–44
  male homosociality within 39, 67–72, 75, 89, 127n19
  nationalism and 66–84
nationalism 27, 65–6
  Afrikaner 6–7
  European 23, 65, 66, 131n1
  German 8–9, 17, 20, 41, 66–84, 124n11
  postcolonial 7, 23–6, 65–7, 101–2, 104–5, 114–15, 131n1
nazi juridical discourse, homosexuality and 9, 29–44
nazi SS 29, 71–2
New Altruism 94, 97
Nuremberg trials 87

oedipal complex 70 79–80, 90, 131n4
Oosterhuis, Harry 39, 40, 41, 131n3
Origins of Totalitarianism (Arendt) 9, 22–3

Paragraph 129 I-b 56–7
Paragraph 175A of Reich Penal Code 124n3
Paragraph 175 of Reich Penal Code 9, 10, 12, 18, 24, 30–1, 34, 37, 45, 52, 71, 86, 87, 123n5, 125n4
Patton, Cindy 94–5, 96, 99, 100, 101
phallus 76–8
political affiliation, sexuality and 11–12, 82–4
population policy 9–10, 17, 33–6, 39, 55, 62
pornography 38
postcolonial nationalism 7, 23–6, 65–7, 101–2, 104–5, 114–15, 131n1
postcolonial world, racialization of sexuality in 9–10, 13, 20, 24, 99–105
Proctor, Robert B. 54, 55, 91, 130n11, 130n12, 137n9
protease inhibitors 97, 98, 136n13
psychoanalysis 11, 12, 73–4, 76, 79–80, 90

queer theory 19–20, 113, 115–16, 120

racial hygiene 8–9, 33–4, 36, 38, 42, 49, 109, 136n1
Reagan, Ronald 94–5, 97
Reich Penal Code 9, 10, 12, 18, 24, 30–1, 34, 35, 37, 45, 52, 54, 56, 71, 117
Reparation Act, German Federal Republic 86–7
repressed homosexuality, *see* latent homosexuality

reproductive futurism 114–17, 137n9
rhetorical democracy 117–18
Rich, Adrienne 128n2
Ringelheim, Joan Miriam 47, 54
Rittner, Carol 15
Robertson, Pat 95
Roellig, Ruth Margarete 48–9, 129n4
Röhm, Ernst 32, 71, 125n7
Röll, Wolfgang 43, 125n10
Rosenfeld, Alvin 111

Said, Edward 69
Sandmann, Gertrude 50
Sartre, Jean-Paul 133n13
Saussurean linguistics 25, 75–6
Schoppmann, Claudia 45–6, 49–51, 53, 55, 56, 57, 60
Schragenheim, Felice 59–60
scientific racism 7, 33–4, 65
Sedgwick, Eve 71, 72, 93
Seel, Pierre 133n1
Sexual Offences and Domestic Violence Act 116
sexuality
    as discursive 19–21
    Foucauldian approaches to 18–21, 75
    political affiliation and 11–12, 82–4
    racialization of 9–10, 12–13, 20, 24, 29–44, 99–105
Shari'a code 105–6
social respectability 36–41, 115–16
Sontag, Susan 94, 99
South Africa 6–7, 22–4, 100–1, 115, 116, 121n3, 136n15
Spurlin, William J., *Imperialism within the Margins* 6, 23, 24, 101, 121n3, 131n1, 136n15, 136n16, 137n6
Stein, Gertrude 82–3
Stimpson, Catharine R. 49
Sullivan, Andrew 97–8, 99

Theweleit, Klaus 11, 68, 70, 79, 127n18
Third Reich 109–10; *see also* National Socialism
 imperialism of 26
Toklas, Alice B. 82–3
totalitarianism 9, 22–4, 26–7, 68, 69
Treatment Action Campaign (TAC) 136n15

United States, homophobia in 88–9, 93, 94, 111, 133n2, 134n3
 HIV/AIDS crisis in 94–6
 Iraq invasion by 119
United States Holocaust Memorial Museum (USHMM) 2, 54
Universal Declaration of Human Rights 105
U.S. Center for Disease Control (CDC) 95

Warner, Michael 113
Weimar Republic 5, 10, 19, 37–8, 48–51, 54, 56, 62, 109, 129n6

Wiesel, Elie 16
Wiesenthal, Simon 16
women; *see also* lesbians
 contemporary homophobia and 105–7
 experience of Holocaust by 46–8
 Jewish 46–7
 masculine identification in 55
 medical discourses on 42
 postcolonial 118–19
 relationships between 54
 restriction of, to domestic sphere 10–11, 41–2, 47, 54–5, 63, 107, 130n10
 as threat 70–1
World Health Organization (WHO) 99, 102–3
World War I 11, 32–3, 67–8, 70, 82
Wright, Elizabeth 76
Wust, Elisabeth 59–60

Zimmermann, Elisabeth 50, 51
Zucker, Kenneth 92

William J. Spurlin
General Editor

This new series is a forum for the investigation and analysis of the contested terrain between culture, gender, and sexuality. Titles in the series can include, but are not limited to, (re)theorizations of gender in relation to, or its constitution through, sexuality, race, class, or culture, studies of sexuality and sexual identity that produce new understandings of gender, or new inquiries into culture, broadly defined, that raise compelling implications for the ways in which we think about gender and sexuality in the contemporary social world. Of particular interest are manuscripts that cirtique and/or broaden traditional constructions of gender and take into account sexuality, race, class, or the pressures of other constitutive categories, analyze nonwestern literary and cultural representations of gender and their relationship to sexuality, especially in postcolonial contexts, and theorize transgender from feminist, queer, postcolonial, or cultural studies frameworks.

For additional information about this series or for the submission of manuscripts, please contact:
> Peter Lang Publishing, Inc.
> 29 Broadway, 18th floor
> New York, New York 10006

To order other books in this series, please contact our Customer Service Department:
> (800) 770-LANG (within the U.S.)
> (212) 647-7706 (outside the U.S.)
> (212) 647-7707 FAX

Or browse online by series:
> www.peterlang.com